Debut of Diversity

Matthew Wiley
2018

Debut of
Diversity

The Emerging Conversation
About Autism and Higher Education

— Matthew Amos Wilson —
M.Ed., M.Div.

Foreword by Emilio Amigo, PhD

©2017 AAPC Publishing
11209 Strang Line Road
Lenexa, Kansas 66215
www.aapcpublishing.net

Publisher's Cataloging-in-Publication

Names: Wilson, Matthew Amos, 1964- author.

Title: Debut of diversity / Matthew Amos Wilson.

Description: Lenexa, Kansas : AAPC Publishing, [2016] | Includes bibliographical references.

Identifiers: ISBN: 978-1-942197-20-1 | LCCN: 2016944695

Subjects: LCSH: Autism spectrum disorders--Patients--Education (Higher) | Autistic people--Education (Higher) | Asperger's syndrome--Patients--Education (Higher) | Counseling in higher education--Handbooks, manuals, etc. | Parents of autistic children--Handbooks, manuals, etc. | College administrators--Handbooks, manuals, etc. | Education, Higher--Social aspects.

Classification: LCC: LB2343 .W55 2016 | DDC: 378.1/98--dc23

Printed in the United States.

To loving Janine,

My apple blossom inspiration,

Summer sunflower joy

Same cane forever friend.

Contents

Foreword

As a young boy I remember being fascinated by marbles and was quite proud of my personal collection. Though I never became much of a skilled or competitive marbles player, I still enjoyed laying them out on the floor and drawing the large arena circle that served as the outer boundary. The hardest part for me was holding the large shooter marble in such a way that I would have the greatest velocity and accuracy. It wasn't until I read Matthew Wilson's book, *Debut of Diversity*, that I remembered how beautifully slick and colorful each marble was and, though exactly the same shape, how unique and individually designed they were, and how beautifully this represents autism.

Matthew Wilson reminds us how people who share core characteristics of autism spectrum disorder (ASD) can still be tremendously diverse and different, much like beautiful marbles can be variegated and unique while belonging to the same set. Matthew has a storyteller's way of reminding us to look more intently at those young adults living with autism, and their individual and collective journey into higher education, in order to lay out a path and a plan to invite academic and personal success.

I am honored to work with Matthew on a daily basis, and I have seen with my own eyes his remarkable ability to connect with and understand both individuals with ASD and their families, and truly take them by the hand to navigate the treacherous waters of the transition years and their daunting challenges. He is a sort of Wizard of Oz, if you will. Not the mysterious and terrifying Great Wizard, but rather the "behind-the-curtain" caring and wise man who knows just what to say and do to help us with our life journey. He takes away the paralyzing fear that hinders most, and replaces it with hope, understanding, and determination to succeed.

From my perspective as a clinician who has developed an ASD social skills therapy group program, I was thrilled to read how important Matthew believes it is for students to fully understand how their own unique form of ASD affects them on a daily basis. This goes far beyond just knowing your diagnosis. This self-awareness and understanding includes related strengths and challenges, and provides a language for seeking and justifying needed supports. Only then can a sense of personal identity be established and provide a foundation for successful self-advocacy.

Having worked for many years in the field of higher education, Matthew effectively challenges educational institutions to powerfully support intellectual differences in such a way that the institution will be strengthened and improved. He delicately points out how this endeavor helps promote truth-seeking and practical wisdom that eventually results in student independence and quality outcomes.

Matthew emphasizes the need to see students with ASD as individuals deserving our respect, care and understanding, and whose personal integrity must always be at the forefront of our purpose and assistance. His approach is very inclusive and validating of our unique human experiences. Without this approach and understanding, no educational institution can form a helpful relationship with their students with ASD.

Debut of Diversity reminds us that we must not stop short of transforming the institution of higher education and demanding academic success for the individual until we have fostered community-wide awareness and understanding, giving birth to a commitment of supporting and celebrating intellectual differences.

With this new way of looking at diversity, I may go hunting around the attic for the marbles I played with as a child. Somehow I think they will look even more magical than they did before.

Dr. Emilio M. Amigo (PSY.D.)
Amigo Family Counseling, LLC

Preface

The first picture arrived the way pictures usually do these days, attached to an email from the proud mother and father. It was not at the best resolution, but there it was, the first of many debuts, many first public appearances. The focus of so many people's hopes and dreams—the first real look at a shiny new baby boy named *Eric*.

As the years go by, we debut again and again. We are born. We take our first step. We say our first word. We walk into our first days of preschool, kindergarten, high school—and college. Most of those special days include a celebration. There are first birthday parties and Sweet Sixteen celebrations. There are first communions and bar and bat mitzvahs. There are driver's licenses, prom pictures, graduations, first jobs, tenureships, and retirement parties. There is the moment that catches in a father's throat when his daughter takes his arm for the long walk down the aisle— *"Be careful of the gloves, Daddy."* We take this all-too-common pattern of first steps and life events almost as a given, a set path for how life is supposed to progress. Sometimes, however, that path of events shifts and takes an unexpected turn.

Soon this happened to Eric. At age three, he was the "boy who doesn't talk like he should." At four, a mystified babysitter told Eric's parents, "All he wanted to do while you were gone is line up his toy cars over and over again." At five, he went to school, and then Eric was introduced to the public as someone new—he debuted as a boy with autism.

When we think of debuts, we often think of the famous ones on television: The Beatles on *The Ed Sullivan Show*, Susan Boyle on *Britain's Got Talent*. Television also has debuted shows that challenged our cultural assumptions about race and disability with shows like *All in the Family*, *Cosby*, and *Ironside*. Recently, the media has also played its part in introducing us to characters and people who have autism. Sometimes the point of these debuts is for the public to learn about autism, as with Temple Grandin's books and appearances. At other times, the word "autism" is not specifically mentioned, but implied. There are now autistic-like lawyers, cops, and scientists. Yet this depiction of autism is not new.

For years, there have been characters awkward in social contexts and lacking strong, long-lasting, or happy emotional connections with others. Beloved "weirdoes" who use limited, often repetitive, speech and who seem to know everything about one or two things, but care nothing for knowing about anything else. We know them by various names: Sherlock Holmes; "Rain Man;" or even "Odd Uncle Ned" who still lives in the spare room over Grandma's garage. If the reason for Uncle Ned's "oddness" is autism, then it is less likely that he ever debuted as a new driver or a nervous groom. His awkward social skills, his poor grasp of the subtleties of language, his perceived narrow interests, and his adherence to routines also probably kept him from becoming a college graduate. This is especially true if he came of age before 1995, when autism became more widely recognized. That year, parent groups started galvanizing academic and political leaders to look at autism and tackle the vicissitudes it brings to all levels of our culture, from family life to education to the workforce.

Autism first came into my life a decade before this when, in 1985, I spent four months doing my practicum at the Developmental Center for Autistic Children (DCAC) in Philadelphia. It took two trains and a bus to get from my house at 43rd and Baltimore, just across from Clark Park, out to Fairmont Park where DCAC was located. DCAC was what we would now call a "pullout" school for the Philadelphia Public School System. There were approximately one hundred fifty students there, three to eleven-years-old. The director, Dr. Bertram Ruttenburg, called them "latency-age" children. They each were diagnosed with autism; everyone I ran into outside of DCAC for the four months I was there, as well as anyone I told about it for the next ten years would ask the same question: "What is autism?" I would answer them with the mantra I learned at the center: language delays, normal intelligence, poor eye contact, low affect, and stereotypical behaviors like twirling, rocking, or flapping. Few would respond with any understanding until after 1988, when I could add, "Did you ever see *Rain Man*?"

Dr. Ruttenburg was the epitome of a psychoanalyst. He was big and white-haired and spoke with an accent. His eyes blazed with enthusiasm, and he used his hands to emphasize his points. There was a determination about him that was difficult to counter, and a gentleness beneath it that was difficult to fathom. The basic treatment plan at the center was hiring mostly young women with high school diplomas to spend time with the children and to, well, love them. They were encouraged to hug and speak with them, and take care of their physical needs. At that time, autism was still recovering from damage done by a book by Bruno Bettelheim titled *The Empty Fortress*. Its premise: autism results from poor parenting or incomplete bonding. Although Bettelheim's "research" was discredited by the time I did my internship in Philadelphia in 1985, the belief remained that by helping children bond with the workers, their other deficits would slowly disappear. I worked with a dozen or so fantastic women that semester. Eventually, I began to understand exactly what the center tried to do with and for the children, using techniques that still impress me, even after all these years.

Down one long dark hall of the building ran a series of one-way mirrors looking into therapy spaces. The students each got time in one of these rooms with an attentive adult. There was a room full of toys for play therapy; a space for art therapy; and a room where, twice a week, a "pet emotive" therapist would come and bring an animal to the students. At the end of the hall of mirrors was a music therapy classroom. In this room, I first encountered a young man who continues to drive my passion for higher education and autism to this day.

Anthony was an eleven-year-old African-American boy in his last year of eligibility for the DCAC. When I first laid eyes on him, he was sitting in front of a keyboard playing. He had headphones on, and smiled broadly as he swayed left and right. Although he was not blind, he looked just like Stevie Wonder, and he *was* truly a wonder. After a few minutes, one of the therapists came up and explained that Anthony wrote music on the keyboard...and not just the occasional childish melody. Nor was it derivative of anything the music therapist had ever heard before. Anthony composed his music by layering it up from a simple tune. The center owned a "high-tech" synthesizer (for the time) that allowed him to record one line and then play it back in the earphones as he accompanied it. In this way, Anthony composed seven- and eight-part music. This boy, with a working vocabulary of twenty-three words, was creating symphonies!

I did not get to work with Anthony as much as I wanted while I was there, primarily because he was being prepared to go back into the Philadelphia school system, or to some other placement that would take over after his twelfth birthday. The professionals who worked with him turned over every leaf to find him a suitable placement, but on the day I left the center, they were still searching.

Even today, I recall heading home on the train for the last time. Anthony, all of the wonderful, mysterious children I had the privilege of working with—their fates moved me to tears. What would become of them? The main thing I found to console myself was that there were not many children diagnosed with autism then. It was a rare condition; not one, they said, that I was likely to encounter again. As a newly minted twenty-one-year-old adult, I believed I would probably never meet another child with autism, and I certainly would never have a person with autism in my family.

The consolation I felt on that train in 1985 did not stand the test of time. Within a year, I became the "big brother" (thanks to the wonderful Big Brothers, Big Sisters program) of another young man with autism. After my time in Philadelphia, I earned a Masters of Divinity from Duke University and became an ordained minister. A variety of children came into my life in the pastorate. I did "Sharing Caring" camps for all manner of children labeled "developmentally disabled," many of whom would have been diagnosed autistic if it were more common then. I eventually left my primary career in the church, earned a Masters of Education, and became an intervention specialist in the public schools. Once again, I had the privilege of working with students on the spectrum—this time in a junior high school. In 1994, the DSM-IV introduced Asperger's syndrome as a form of autism (American Psychiatric Association). Unlike Anthony and his schoolmates, society began to find a place for students with autism beyond elementary school, but it was still a ways away from directing them toward higher education.

Finally, in 2007 and 2008, two things happened to refocus my attention on individuals with autism. My grandson, born in 2004, quite suddenly lost much of his acquired vocabulary and speech. In the spring of 2007, my son and daughter-in-law took him to the doctor, and, as is the case for many children on the spectrum, we initially thought a problem with his tonsils caused his symptoms, and then perhaps a hearing problem. He had an operation to insert tubes in his ears, which helped, but his other symptoms did not go away. In June, he was diagnosed with pervasive developmental disorder, not otherwise specified (PDD-NOS), a catchall diagnosis in the DSM-IV-TR (American Psychiatric Association, 1993) that included atypical autism. After a more complete evaluation, the doctor diagnosed him with autism.

Just as we were coming to terms with this in our family, a regional educational service center contacted me to start a transition program for students on the spectrum at a large community college. I was very excited about the position and soon realized that I was well suited for it. I never thought of myself as an educational entrepreneur, but when presented with the opportunity to clear the way for my own grandson, as well as the army of school-age autistic children like him, to attend college one day, I would give it a shot.

Introduction

Why a book of stories on autism and higher education?

For the past ten or fifteen years, the early diagnosis of autism spectrum disorders (ASDs) has increased rapidly in the United States and other Western nations. In the United States, the wave of younger children with autism is piling up as it reaches institutions of higher education. There is very little nationally representative data on youth with autism between high school age and the early twenties.

The A.J. Drexel Autism Institute at Drexel University is the first institution to look at autism in this age group from a public health perspective, rather than on an individual basis. Their Life Course Outcomes Research looks at adult indicators with nationally representative data from two surveys, the 2009 National Longitudinal Transition Study-2 and the 2011 Survey of Pathways to Diagnosis (Roux, 2015). This effort, by its own accounting, has a couple of limitations. First, the Survey of Pathways to Diagnosis missed young adults on the spectrum who do not have mental health issues, as well as those who may be unaccounted-for because they have a milder or undiagnosed form of ASD. Second, only 30% of the respondents were adults with autism who reported for themselves. The study looked at several factors, including mental health, social isolation, community involvement, and independent living. For purposes of this discussion, the following indicators explain where the United States falls in terms of students with autism in higher education.

A few of the major findings follow:

- 26% of young adults received no services in their early twenties
- 36% attended some type of postsecondary education, and 70% of attendees went to two-year colleges (even though most programs for autistic students are at four-year colleges)
- 37% were disconnected from both work and education after high school
- All of these percentages were even lower for low-income students and students of color

The Drexel Report is the only nationally applicable research on autism indicators to date (Roux, 2015). Much ground remains to be covered in relation to autism and higher education across the United States, but we can already feel the impact of students with autism coming to higher education.

Students on the Spectrum at Columbus State Community College

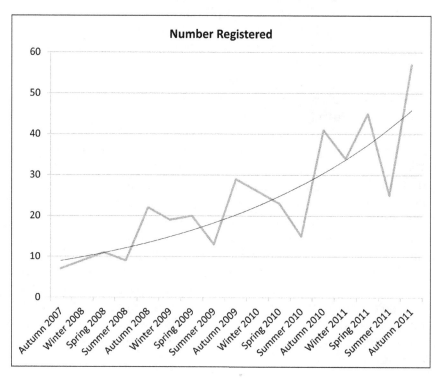

For instance, in Ohio, Columbus State Community College students identifying themselves as on the autism spectrum went up 700% between the autumn of 2007 and the autumn of 2011 (see figure). The total percentage of students served by this community college's disability services department that year raised to 5.5% autistic—out of nearly 1,000. Schools across Ohio seem to reflect this trend.

A 2012 survey of 18 Ohio higher-education facilities reported 251 students on the autism spectrum—an average of 13.9 students per institution, with the median being 4 (Wilson & McClane, 2012). I believe that more research will demonstrate the need for high school graduates with autism to have postsecondary school opportunities. Like other states, Ohio tracks what its public high school graduates are doing one year after graduation. In Ohio, only 6% of graduates with autism hold competitive employment; 32% are in two- to four-year postsecondary schools; and 14% are attempting to both hold down a job and attend college (Filler, 2010).

It is clear that college and university disability services providers must continue to discover how best to tailor the services they offer to the rising ASD population. Students on the spectrum and higher education institutions would both benefit from sharing information with one another about creating programs that welcome students and ensure they have the very best access possible to earning degrees.

This book brings together stories of people with autism and their allies in hopes that program creation and information-sharing can keep pace with the growing number of students on the spectrum entering postsecondary education. Each chapter begins with an aphorism, or "foundation," relating autism to college success. Chapters 1–7 focus on student growth and achievement. Chapters 8–10 focus on institutional philosophy and transformation.

STRUCTURE OF THIS BOOK

The Foundations of Autism and Academic Success

Part One: The Student

Preparation: Key to a successful debut as a college student is getting the student and her or his allies involved in the preparation plan the summer before—most of all, putting the student in charge of the plan as the first day approaches.

Developmental Stages: An 18-year-old on the spectrum is still an 18-year-old. Many young adults find themselves still working through developmental stages; therefore, when allies coach competence, fidelity, and love, students both on and off the spectrum may come to understand and accept who they are and that others want to help them grow.

Competence: Rhetorically speaking, time is one of the student's only commodities; make time for time (management). Teaching students how to master their time in their own way is the ally's most important task.

Identity: Allies should respect adult students, and students should claim their identity but be realistic about strengths and academic challenges, *and seek support.*

Intimacy: A program or an ally can provide tools to unmask the "hidden curriculum," but in the end, the student has to open up, and seek out friends and dates on his or her own terms, and learn to cooperate with his or her instructors.

Accommodations: Colleges and universities may provide additional accommodations that do not deal directly with academic success. Finding accommodations that work for people on the spectrum is still a work in progress.

Two Models: Students achieve success in higher education by learning their own data at intake to determine how ASD will affect them academically, then using that information to shape the way they approach their certificate or degree program.

Part Two: The Institution

Truth: Institutions base effective support of intellectual differences on seeking truth with practical wisdom that promotes independence and quality outcomes.

Research: Students are more than what the research suggests.

Transformation: Transforming the academy and changing the academic success rate of students with autism requires awareness within an entire higher education community and commitment to supporting intellectual differences.

* * *

Each chapter contains three interrelated sections. Chapters begin with a narrative drawn from a first-person experience, a formal writing, a case study, or an illustration. These examples demonstrate what autism looks like in a college context. A reflection on the example then follows. In order to encourage groups of students and higher education professionals to read and discuss this book together, each chapter ends with another illustrative story and a set of discussion questions exploring the themes of the chapter.

Although I have included specific writings from students and their allies (like "I'm an Autistic Kid When I'm at Disneyland"), in order to protect the specific identities of students and their allies, the characters in the text (e.g., "Sally," "Wade," and "Eric") are amalgams of many different people I have worked with over the years. Just as dentists use filling material to strengthen and preserve the whole tooth, these characters "fill in" the gaps for readers. The issues in these stories are real issues that autistic students in the academy raise. Please read them in such a light and know that, just as no one person is the epitome of a person with autism, no one character can cover the diversity of real people who face these challenges in colleges and universities every day.

AUTISM SPECTRUM DISORDER

Word by Word

Expanding on the three parts of the name *autism—spectrum—disorder* reveals essential information for working with young adults on the spectrum.

First, no matter where the DSM leads, the world has come to regard the term *autism* as something that is an observable reality. As with most diagnoses, time and experience help us refine our definition of human behavior, and time will continuously change the way we look at autism; however, the definition Tony Attwood offers is an excellent place to start. Attwood (2006) wrote in *The Complete Guide to Asperger's Syndrome* that autism is "a neurological disorder that affects one's ability to understand and respond to others' thoughts and feelings." Key to this definition is that autism is *neurological*, which says a great deal about the perceived motivations behind the behavior of students with ASD.

In workshops I have conducted, I have emphasized that students on the spectrum are not *choosing* to be stubborn, argumentative, disorganized, klutzy, or antisocial. Educators who accept the neurological basis for their students' frustrating or baffling behavior are going to be more successful in mentoring the student to achieve. Instructors who choose to ignore the neurological connection in their dealings with students on the spectrum will only frustrate themselves and their students when it comes to achieving success in the classroom.

The second word in the overall label, *spectrum*, may be defined as "having autistic characteristics that run the range from mild (looks like shyness) to extreme (complete aloofness)." Lorna Wing first introduced this term by explaining that all of our characteristics, not just our autistic ones, fall across a spectrum. People on the spectrum themselves, as well as those who work with them, must bear in mind that all characteristics of humans are subject to "the drag of the bell curve." The concept of a spectrum is central to the literature about autism and the way those who have autism think of themselves.

Several of my students came to me believing that they were "brilliant"; few of my students, however, have actually been geniuses. One of the myths of the ASD stereotype is that if a person on the spectrum is not socially competent, it is acceptable because they are, after all, so much smarter than everyone else. The truth is that most people, both on and off the autism spectrum, have varying skills and levels of giftedness. Not everyone with Asperger's syndrome looks like Bill Gates (who incidentally has not ever confirmed that he has Asperger's syndrome); in fact, no one looks like Bill Gates *except* for Bill Gates. The real key to success in young adulthood is for students to discover who they are, with their own sets of unique gifts and challenges, and then for them to build their life choices around that reality.

The final word of the label is *disorder*, and here is where controversy arises. We generally define it as "a collection of symptoms." Much of the grist of our psychological mill comes from looking for, analyzing, and expanding upon observable symptoms of psychiatric distress or differences from the "norm." The problem with the "D" in ASD, however, is the negative connotations now associated with it. In the world of psychoanalysis and therapy, "disorder" is a perfectly suitable appellation, but among some of those who are on the spectrum, or sensitive to those they know, love, or work with on the spectrum, "disorder" is no longer acceptable. We removed other diagnostic words like "idiot," "lunatic" and "retarded" from the lexicon of disability. It may follow that "disorder" is also on its way out.

Just as other diagnostic words like "depression" and "hyperactivity" lost their specificity once they gained popularity, "autism" looks different today because of its depiction in popular media. The term "autistic" now transcends the original DSM definition. Just as it was once difficult to separate autism from Dustin Hoffman's interpretation in *Rain Man*, the "autistic-like character" has made its way onto nearly every TV screen. The range of real characters in the public eye spans from the ubiquitous and inspiring Temple Grandin to the alarming images of twirling disconnected autistic children in commercials meant to stimulate our pity and encourage us to give money to autism charities.

This plethora of images does not make it easier to see the person beneath the symptoms, nor the people in our day-to-day lives who live with autism. Though I have never been diagnosed with autism myself, I recognize the trap that Anne Donnellon humorously pointed out when she said, "Sometimes I think that what most unites people on the autism spectrum is how they affect the rest of us," (Autistic Self-Advocacy Network, 2011). Amid all the imagery, it is essential that we allow room for those who *are* on the spectrum to seek and refine the definition of "autism." This effort is especially important for college students to address, for it is their developmental business to be about the work of individuation and self-definition.

Finally, for purposes of this book, I will use both the more traditional "people/person on the spectrum" and the term "autistic(s)." The latter comes from the many people on the spectrum who prefer to sacrifice the person-first language in favor of simply calling themselves "autistics."

We summarily describe the phenomenon of autism as a relationship problem caused by a misunderstanding of social reciprocity. Though at first this may seem to take in the totality of the diagnosis, it fails to recognize an essential piece of the definition of reciprocity. If I label someone by saying, "You are an autistic person who doesn't know how to relate to me," then what about my also not relating to them? Relationships begin when we hear one another's story. One of the best ways to handle reciprocity is to include the voices of those who are on the spectrum. This book seeks to include the stories of people with autism, as well as the higher education professionals with whom they work. Perhaps some of these stories will contribute to a better appreciation of autism and encourage more opportunities for those who live, work, and go to school with autism.

PART I

The Student

Preparation

Getting Ready for the Debutante Ball

Very few parts of society still hold a debutante ball. If they do, I suspect that most autistics would not be caught dead at such an event. Despite the irony, a parallel exists between students with autism going to college, and the old tradition of a "coming-out party" for young women in high society. (Watch the documentary *How to Dance In Ohio* by Gidalya Pictures, chronicling a prom-style dance that several Ohio students from Amigo Family Counseling took part in.) Both situations involve young people brought into the society of adults with certain social expectations. Elders carefully instruct debutantes about how to "be" in public. They practice social manners prior to the event. To some extent, the opportunities open to the debutantes in the future depend upon how well each performs at the party.

This may also be the case for students with autism as they come into the college environment. Many of them attended Applied Behavior Analysis (ABA) therapy or some other form of behavioral treatment as a child. For some, schools may have introduced them to social skills training or speech therapy while in middle or high school. Families and friends often labor with their autistic children for years over how to behave in public. Perhaps mom, dad, and other specially trained adults have accompanied the student through school to help them find ways to perform and succeed.

When they come to college as a young adult, they are ready to make their public debut on their own—or at least as ready as their allies and loved ones can make them. Nevertheless, the moment they step into the admissions office or take their seat in that first college class, they are as subject as any other debutante to making that perfect first impression. Opportunities from that day forward may depend on how well they do the first day of class, and how well they do may rely on how well they have been prepared and coached for the experience. A two- or four-year higher education experience is a social proving ground, not just vocational preparation.

The next section introduces three students and describes the different directions their individual debuts took them. Sally attended college right after high school, which attempted to prepare her. Eric's preparation was more in-depth and included some preliminary assessment. Jacob debuted with an unrealistic understanding of his abilities and very little preparation for the demands of college.

SALLY

One high school program for autistic students excelled in anticipating what skills and abilities its students would need to master before reaching college. They measured those abilities in their students and found one group, including a girl named Sally, whom they thought were most capable of doing well. They then spent an entire term preparing them to succeed. They helped them choose courses, taught them how to register for those courses online, coached them in ways to control the anxiety and stress that might result from being in the new campus environment, and even provided transportation to the college.

A week after the big day had come and gone, Sally's father reported that his daughter had come home visibly happy, which was an unusual thing for her. When he asked about her experiences at school, he learned that she had only gone to class once all week. She told him that on the first day, she was unable to find her medieval history classroom. After wandering in terror and confusion for the first two days, she finally found the room. However, after attending the class on the third day, she decided it was a waste of time. The professor didn't say one thing about Druidism, even when she specifically asked him to do so. On the fifth day, she came home happy because she finally found a place on campus where she could sit in peace and use the college facilities she needed to do her own research on Druidism. After all, she reminded her father, studying Druidism was the reason she chose the medieval history class in the first place, and she already learned several new things about it at college in just one day, despite what she called her "unfocused professor."

This scenario describes a fairly typical first week for a college student with ASD. I have students who made similar decisions about their classes or professors well into the semester and even beyond their first year of college. The DSM-5 diagnosis for autism notes that people on the spectrum have deficits in social approach (how to begin a conversation or approach a social setting) that limit their ability to rescue themselves from a situation like not finding a classroom (American Psychiatric Association, 2013). A neurotypical (any person not on the spectrum) individual might simply ask for directions to class when lost, but a person on the spectrum might not. Furthermore, the diagnosis notes that a highly restricted interest (like Druidism) may override other considerations (like going to class) in the mind of a young college student with autism. For Sally, her choices made perfect sense, but for her Dad, not so much.

For students with autism, it is possible to be derailed in many ways in the first few days of college, but they do not always grasp that this happens. Sally's allies (including her well-meaning high school program) could have improved her chances to shine during her first week by doing three things. First, students often need more than just one school term to work on the characteristics, skills, or domains that challenge them. Doing this work in the college setting is always preferable to doing it while still in the high school classroom, hence why many programs for autistics use the label "college-based transition." Many potential impediments to success exist for a newly-minted college student with autism. One of them is hyper- and hyporeactivity to sensory input, which may cause the student to spend a lot of mental energy on just getting used to the looks, feels, smells, and even tastes associated with the new environment. Using so much energy on the environment does not leave much for focus on studies. College is full of many different forms of sensory input that are not found in high school. Even if sensory issues are well regulated in a high school student, the college environment may challenge them with its novelty and new set of demands. Thus, Sally's allies from her high school might have also provided an on-site college coach to help her get used to the college scene before classes started and provide services for her in the college environment once she got there.

What was correct about Sally's experience is that her allies were included in her debut. This is essential for higher education institutions to do. Even though the law considers 18-year-olds to be adults, they are not yet fully independent adults. Parents, former teachers, important adults in their lives, and sometimes even friends and siblings may all contribute to the success of the student's collegiate debut. Including these allies is essential, but it is better if they are included in a systematic way, and several tools are available for doing just that.

ERIC

Including Allies: A Snapshot of Eric from Three Points of View

Before coming to college, students can use the Autism View Rating (AVR) assessment (see Appendix for a blank version). This tool compares the student's self-assessment of specific skills that lead to college success with the assessments of others in his or her life. This kind of tool goes a long way toward predetermining how a student might do on the first day of college. If a student on the spectrum self-discloses his or her diagnosis to an intake specialist or to admissions personnel, then those professionals can have measures like these available for the prospective student. An eighteen-year-old may not want to do this, for reasons discussed later in the book, but let us begin by talking again about Eric, the boy diagnosed in the preface. He and his allies agreed to do the AVR during his last month of high school. It turns out that this choice helped him avoid what happened to Sally.

Eric, his mom, his teacher, and a family friend each filled out a rating form independently. The form consists of twenty-one skills in seven broad categories of three skills each. The categories are Social Skills, Sensory Issues, Time Management, Self-Advocacy, Thinking Style, Organization, and Flexibility. Each respondent was asked to "rate the student's level of skill in the following areas."

They marked the student with a 5 (always); 4 (usually); 3 (sometimes); 2 (almost never); or 1 (no information). The skills and the categories within them were created by a small group of professors with experience teaching students on the autism spectrum. The goal of the tool is to improve the approach to bringing students with autism into higher education. Individual institutions, or even Individualized Education Program (IEP) teams, can elect to adapt the system in their own way. Eric's example follows (Fig. 1.1).

FIG 1.1   Eric's Autism View Rating Sheet Composite

Section 1				
Student Name: Eric				
KEY: S = Student Self-Rating; P = Parent Rating (mom); T = Teacher Rating; O = Other				
Section 2				
Please rate level of skill in the following areas:	**Always (5)**	**Usually (4)**	**Sometimes (3)**	**Almost Never (2)**	**No Info. (1)**
Social Skills				
Waits turn to speak		SPTO			
Participates in small groups successfully	O	SPT			
Respects others' opinions	T	SPO			
Sensory Issues				
Stays in one place throughout structured time	PTO		S		
Is NOT distracted by environment	SO	PT			
Manages own sensory needs appropriately	O	SPT			
Time Management				
Is prompt to class or appointments	PTO	S			
Meets deadlines	STO	P			
Creates and follows schedules	SPTO				

FIG. 1.1 *(continued)*

Section 2					
Please rate level of skill in the following areas:	Always (5)	Usually (4)	Some- times (3)	Almost Never (2)	No Info. (1)
Self-Advocacy					
Expresses him/her self with confidence		STO		P	
Seeks assistance when unsure or confused		STO		P	
States opinions and relays needs clearly		TO	S	P	
Thinking Style					
Handles constructive criticism well		SPTO			
Knows how he/she learns best		SPTO			
Thinks concretely	O	T	SP		
Organization					
Files papers and assignments routinely	TO	S	P		
Finds items quickly when needed or asked	TO	SP			
Breaks large tasks into small, workable parts	O	T	S	P	
Flexibility					
Sets obtainable goals	T	O	S	P	
Independently makes short-term decisions	T	O	SP		
Adapts to a change of routine effectively		T	SPO		

The administrator compares and contrasts the four respondents' rating forms to see if patterns emerge. For instance, is there congruence (positive or negative) among all four raters on any one category? Is there a broad disparity? If so, in what categories and between which raters? Does the student hold a different view of his or her abilities than all three of his or her allies do? Is it possible to notice certain items or categories that the teacher sees at school, but the parent does not see at home, or vice versa. The most important outcome of the system is helping students determine their level of college readiness. What are the strengths they have that will help them in college? What challenges can they address before college starts?

An interesting picture of Eric emerged from this process. A quick look at the entire chart (see Fig. 1.2) indicates that all of the ratings for Eric are generally higher and more congruent in the first three categories (Social Skills, Sensory Issues, and Time Management) than they are in the last four.

Time management is clearly Eric's biggest strength. All of his allies agree. Many students with autism find this set of skills a challenge (remember Sally?), but not Eric. Additionally, since Eric does well sitting through the longer classes at school, he does not need to shy away from registering for those two- or three-hour-long courses that can sometimes destroy a less patient, more anxious student. Eric's strengths will help him in college. However, the numbers also reveal some other interesting aspects of Eric's college readiness.

Positive Congruence

On what skills do all of the respondents, including Eric, agree? For instance, all three skills of the Time Management category show a high positive congruence. All four respondents, including Eric himself, agree he "always" (rating of 5) "creates and follows schedules." Three out of four agreed Eric "is prompt to class and appointments" and he "meets deadlines." Apparently, Eric is good at managing his time, and he knows it. Two of the skills in the Thinking Style category also have a high positive congruence. Eric and his allies all agreed that he "usually" (4) "handles constructive criticism well" and that he "knows how he learns best." Finally, three out of four respondents gave Eric a (5), or "Always," for "stays in one place during structured time." All of these skills are Eric's strengths because of the high positive congruency they received from all four respondents.

Negative Congruence

Congruency can also be negative. For instance, although Eric does not have any skill area where all respondents report low scores (2 or 3), this may mean there is no skill that is clearly a weakness or

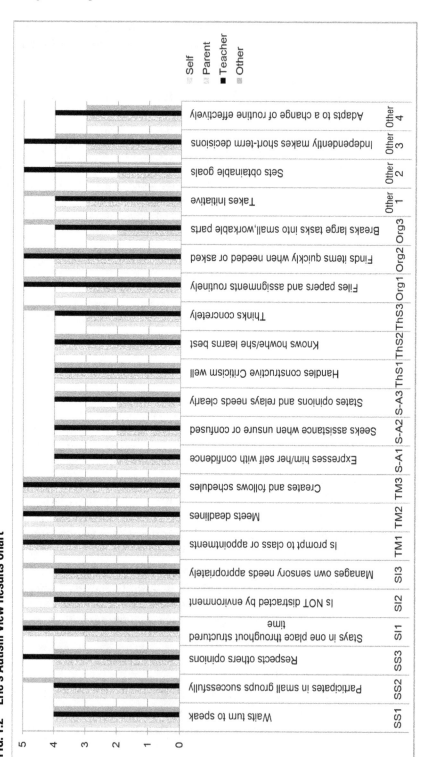

FIG. 1.2   Eric's Autism View Results Chart

deficit, or it may mean that the tool does not have a skill on it that corresponds to a deficit area where Eric struggles. If this is the case, it may also indicate that this is an unrealistic picture of Eric. No tool is perfect. That is why I encourage allies and professionals to adapt the AVR system of data collection to their own expectations and student clientele.

Incongruence

The administrator also analyzes the data for incongruence. Incongruity is found whenever a skill or category demonstrates a broad range of responses. This can happen when one person gives the student a (2) on a skill set, a second person a (3), and the third a (4). In this case, the range is 3. Determining causation for incongruence is difficult, but it may open up several places where the student and his allies can start a discussion about his or her college readiness. Eric's data include several incongruent skills, such as "breaks tasks into small workable parts" and "sets obtainable goals." The next step in the process involves talking to Eric, his mom, and the others about the areas where their responses vary widely. The administrator does this in a series of follow-up interviews.

The follow-up interviews have two goals. First, the student's strengths and readiness for college are celebrated. Second, the group discusses the reasons why the student and his allies rated the skills differently from one another. The student is encouraged to stay in charge of this dialogue and to find ways to accept the incongruent skills as possible challenge areas and to bring those disparate skills into sync during the summer months before college begins. Eric's AVR results seem to indicate the following overall pattern: Eric's mother consistently rates Eric lower than the other respondents in many of the broadly ranging skills. Why is this? Could it be that she has less faith in his readiness than necessary, or is it that she is right about Eric, and he is overconfident? Eric, his teacher, and his neighbor all rate him higher in these same categories, so might it be that he does better at school and in the community than he does at home? What role does "letting go" play in the dynamic between Eric and his mom? More information comes out of the follow-up interview questions. Here are some typical responses that respondents give during this informal one-on-one time with the coach or professional.

When the administrator interviewed Eric's mom, her main concerns rested squarely in the category of self-advocacy. This is typical of parental response:

> I'm just worried that he will not go up and talk to his professors if things start to go bad; that he won't come and talk to me either. Ever since he was a little kid, he refused to talk to me when something bad happens. He would get picked on, and I would hear about it from one of his friends, but not from Eric. I guess that is my main concern, that and that he doesn't set obtainable goals for himself. He often is kind of "pie in the sky" about what he is going to do next, or he won't set any kind of goal at all. That worries me too.

Eric's teacher noted this:

> Eric has always done a commendable job on class assignments—I am a tech teacher, and he loves the computer, so that may be why he does so well. But either way, Eric engages the project every time, and though he is not the most talkative kid in class, when it comes to the project, he will raise his hand and go for it with me. I think that as long as he has a class he likes in college, he will do fine—probably even better than fine.

The "other" rater on the AVR can provide a good insight into how a student will do with new people in novel environments or situations. Usually, this person is a coach or teacher from an extracurricular activity or, as in Eric's case, a family friend. She writes of Eric,

> I am both Eric's neighbor and his first clarinet teacher. I have watched Eric grow up next-door and always found him to be an inspiration. There were times when no one was sure he would break free and join the world—but over time, not only did he join the world, but he did it with vigor and joy. I have watched him go from playing in the sandbox oblivious of his surroundings to playing in the senior band concert last December. Wow! I have done my best to capture this young man in your numbers, but I have so much more to say. I wish him the best of luck in college.

Eric seems to ramble when asked about how he thinks he will do in college: "I'm not sure what I want to do in college, yet—but I think that I will do OK. I'm worried about the other students, the campus—you know, getting around it—and whether I can take a welding class. I really want to learn to weld. But I guess that it will be OK."

Eric and his Allies Develop a Solid Approach to his First Semester

The result of all the analysis of Eric's AVR was setting up two summer meetings with Eric and his coach before college started.

Meeting One: During the first meeting, the coach helped Eric use the AVR results to discover and list his strengths and challenges:

Strengths (informed by positive congruent skills and follow-up talks)

1. I am prompt to appointments and classes.
2. I can handle sitting through long (boring) classes.
3. I really know how to make a schedule AND stick to it!
4. I learn best by listening and drawing things out.
5. I ask for help when I need it (and I promise Mom that I will keep this up).

Challenges (informed by incongruent—broadly ranging skills and follow-up talks)

1. I get overwhelmed by the idea of having to take classes I don't like (English Composition), and I really want to take welding.
2. I can improve my ability to "state opinions and relay needs clearly."
3. I am dreading Freshman Tutorial because I don't like having to choose a "partner" or a group to do anything with, especially something as important as studying!

Meeting Two: While Mom stayed in the waiting room, Eric and his coach drew up a summer plan based on the challenges he listed during the first meeting. Then they invited Mom back into the meeting so that Eric could present his plan. Here is how he planned to address the first challenge he wrote up during meeting one:

"I get overwhelmed by the idea of having to take classes I don't like (English Composition), and I really want to take welding."

1. I will "open my ears" at the summer meetings and really think through what is said before setting up my freshman classes and goals.

2. Coach will periodically ask me to repeat what he says in order to make sure that I understand what general education courses I need to take (annoying! But I won't complain to him).

3. I will not register until Mom and coach agree with my class choices. Here is our compromise:

   a. One required class I can handle with support (boo, Freshman Composition) and

   b. One class I want to take if it is available at registration (yay, Welding!)

This action plan came mostly from information the teacher offered about Eric's motivation. She said that he did well in classes that he liked. In case the opposite is also true, Eric will have to learn to accept the idea that college requires several general courses that may or may not motivate him. This is difficult for anyone to accept, but it is a fact of being a college student. So, during the months leading up to the first day of classes, Eric learned which classes are basic requirements—usually courses with titles like "Freshman Composition" or "College Algebra." He registered his complaints about the whole idea of mandatory classes, and he did his best to accept the fact that they are part of college life anyway. The coach helped him discover the different kinds of support that exist on campus to help students get through Freshman Composition. These helps included a writing center, a tiered set of composition courses based on starting ability, tutors, and study groups.

The allies a student chooses to be part of his summer preparation can add a lot to the success of the student in their new college setting. In Eric's case, his teacher helped him address challenge number one, his mother helped him address challenge number two, and his neighbor provided not only a glimpse of how Eric does in a setting outside of home or school but also how he is perceived by an "outsider." All of their words provided encouragement and inspiration for Eric. They helped him feel confident in three different settings so he could become independent on the college campus.

Eighteen can be a complicated age, and students vary wildly in their level of maturity coming into college. Eric seemed to have a good grasp of his own abilities, as did his allies; however, not all students do, and not all allies are in touch either. One benefit of the

AVR is that if a student does not yet know him- or herself, this will likely show up because they went through the process.

Eric's First Week

Because Eric attended a ten-day intensive orientation to his college (see "Orientation Week" in Chapter 7), by the time he walked into his first day of classes, he had already been on campus a half dozen times or more. He had registered for two classes (not a full load, but enough to get started). They were Freshman Composition and Welding 1. He knew the locations of his classes and had walked to the rooms and mapped out his first week's schedule. Eric had also diligently worked on a script to use when he talked to his Freshman Tutorial teacher (see page 75 for an example of a student-written script).

On the first day of class, he made himself raise his hand and ask the English professor a question about the syllabus. He stayed after the welding class and chatted with the professor every day. When he got home each night, he and his mom agreed that they would spend ten minutes talking about how class went that day. Eric was not too thrilled about this, but he put the ten minutes on his schedule nonetheless. By the end of the week, Eric had attended each class, and he was full of opinions about the professors and their skills. He did not "like" the English teacher, but then, he had not turned in his writing sample yet. On the other hand, Eric was sure that his welding teacher "hung the moon" (which he actually had—in the library's faculty/student art exhibit).

JACOB

In contrast to Eric, a student named Jacob literally rated himself a (5), or "Always," on 21 of the 22 skills. This was not the case for any of his allies. Subsequent interviews showed two things. First, they showed a student who was not realistic about his own abilities. Second, the interviews showed that the student's allies were dismissive of the student and only marginally supportive of him going to college. As sad as this discovery was, it only underscored the likelihood of Jacob not being able to make it in college—yet. Often, systemic issues like an out-of-balance family system, comorbid mental health issues, and issues related to economics can find their way into the results. All this may be considered as data (not reason to judge) to guide the student. In Jacob's case, he and his family were encouraged to postpone his entry into college, and they were directed into other avenues of support. It is important to note that not all students (whether autistic or neurotypical) are ready for college just because they graduate from high school. Other paths are available for a young person to take. Furthermore, even when a young student is not ready for college, they may be eventually. Community colleges enroll many second- or even third-career adults who return for a degree once their experience and/or maturity brings them back around. Jacob chose to go to a career counselor and actually seemed relieved, in the end, that he was introduced to another set of possibilities for his future.

Not every student transition will be as fluid as Eric's will. The best approach to the first year of college includes coordinated input from allies and information about the student in the months or weeks leading up to the first day of classes. However, in the end, the student has to be the primary expert on him- or herself.

QUESTIONS

1. What gets in the way of students on the spectrum preparing for college during the summer before it starts? Do you think that arranging such preparation time is important? Why or why not?

2. The AVR data-gathering system is based on the premise that there should be a balance between respecting the adult status of freshmen and including the students' allies in their preparation for college. Take turns talking about whether you think that this premise was honored in the Eric illustration. Would you, as either an ally or a student on the spectrum, agree to go through the process? What things about the process would sway you toward doing it? What things would dissuade you?

3. In your opinion, what is the difference between a well-meaning ally and a truly helpful, effective one?

Developmental
Stages

E ric is an amalgam of several college students on the spectrum I
have known, loved, and worked with. All of my 18- to 22-year-old college students have taught me one thing: an 18-year-old college student on the spectrum *is still an 18-year-old*. Despite the fact that parents, teachers, siblings, and classmates all know this about their "Erics" and "Ericas," they still can forget this in the rush to label, justify, or authenticate our interactions with one another. Even autistic people and their allies forget it sometimes, especially if they are trying to make a salient point about how autism affects college success. When allies coach toward competence, fidelity, and love, students understand and accept who they are and that others want to help them grow. The work of Erik Erikson gives us a common point to begin to discuss what it means to be both an 18-year-old, and an 18-year-old on the spectrum.

COACHING TOWARD
COMPETENCE, FIDELITY, AND LOVE

In the seminal work on his theories of psychosocial development, extended and completed by his wife and longtime collaborator,

Joan, Erik Erikson delineated that eight main "stages" make up the pattern of human life from infancy through old age (Erikson & Erikson, 1997). Each of these stages contains a focus (or "crisis") that is the result of the person's interaction with the friction in the world around them, and his or her own drives or instincts. These crises are defined by two opposing resolutions, and people most often "resolve" each stage by settling someplace between the two, and also continuously move on to the next stage while sometimes reaching back into an earlier stage or forward into an emerging one.

In Erikson's design, college-age people have moved through the first three stages of development (hope, will, and purpose) and now live among stages four, five, and six. These three stages are characterized by different sets of developmental tasks. Students have (for the most part) resolved stage four, *industry vs. inferiority*, and are working through stages five and six, *identity vs. role confusion* and *intimacy vs. isolation*. The three words Erikson used to describe each stage were *competency* (stage four), *fidelity* (stage five), and affiliational *love* (stage six). When a person takes responsibility for competency, fidelity, and love in his or her life, then he or she has resolved that stage (Erikson & Erikson, p. 54).

Erikson's theoretical constructs apply quite admirably to the world of higher education students. Most young people come to college with a set of questions on their minds. For example, "Am I smart enough to pass my courses?" (Competence). When faced with a new environment where everything is different from what they are used to, they ask, "What/who am I, and what/who will I choose to become?" (Fidelity). A question not far from any young person's mind is "With whom will I associate, and to whom shall I give my heart?" (Affiliation/Love).

Developmental psychology has its limitations, of course. Much of the work has roots in the early 20th century worldview. As a result, it does not take into account essential aspects of humanity that have been more thoroughly described since that time, such as gender, race, ethnicity, sexual orientation, and the effect of intellectual differences in human development. Developmental psychology has not been revised to account for what has been learned about brain anatomy and physiology and about modern genetics. Still, most higher education practitioners and their students benefit from applying principles such as stages, crises, and resolutions to their common quest for academic and social success during the college years. That is why the best faculty, counselors, coaches, and staff realize that questions stemming from these three stages are constantly in the background when they are working with students. Although autistic students may show a proclivity to need extra help in certain aspects of, say, resolving the intimacy vs. isolation stage, much of the coaching we can do does not necessarily need to be specialized for autistics. Sometimes a lonely or isolated student is just that, a lonely or isolated student, and though their autism may exacerbate the loneliness, the techniques we can offer them may not particularly relate to autism. Even neurotypical kids can be confused, even frightened, by their first encounter with the "college lifestyle," as the story at the end of this chapter illustrates. So how does a higher education professional begin to sort out the effects of the autism diagnosis from the effects of the developmental stages through which their students are working?

Competence

Stage four is resolved when a person finds a level of competence in his or her life and work. It has often been resolved by the time a person is fourteen years old; however, introducing someone to the rigor and novelty of an environment like college is likely to stir up issues related to industry vs. inferiority. In the case of autistic students, further complications may arise if they have received messages throughout their K–12 years that amount to "you will not make it in college." Such messages are hard for students to avoid completely, even if they have a supportive family and IEP team. Even when children are identified early and receive services, peers, the media, and even society itself can become the source from which students hear that they are "not college material." Federal and state laws focusing on "least-restrictive environment" mandates have reduced the likelihood of such traps; however, they still happen (see Chapter 6 for further discussion of least-restrictive environments).

The first year we started our campus-based program, one student who came to us was a complete surprise. Initially, the student looked into a job/life skills program designed for persons with developmental disabilities, not autism. In the course of the student's intake meeting, the team decided that his lifelong placement in a multiple disabilities classroom had been the best that the district could offer, but it also blinded the IEP team to the student's potential for college. They placed the young man in the brand-new transition program for students on the spectrum. In the course of his transition year, he earned a "B" average in several developmental courses designed to bring freshmen up to college level. After leaving the program, the student continued to earn a "B" average in the introductory college courses. Eventually, he elected to stop taking classes in favor of taking a job that he described as "work I like, with benefits!" He was the first in his family to attend any college, and much of the confidence that helped propel him into his first job was the result of time he spent learning how to take college classes.

In the end, not every student will choose to go to college or to do so on their parents' timeline. In modern U.S. higher education, people do not have to earn their degree between the ages of eighteen and twenty-two anymore. Community colleges are rife with "nontraditional" students, people retraining for their careers, and people returning to continue their degree. All of these options are open to students on the spectrum as well.

The important caveat to bear in mind is that not all students will find that college is the place where their competence appears—not everyone will benefit from college. This is not just a matter of IQ; often, it stems from a more elusive collection of traits called college "readiness." Readiness consists of emotional maturity, response to environmental conditions, family dynamics and expectations, financial resources, and executive functioning abilities. As Abraham Maslow's (1962) hierarchy of needs reminds us, before someone can fulfill their educational potential, they must first feel safe in their home environment and secure in knowing their physical and emotional needs are met. As teachers and coaches, we can only do so much to assist them in gaining and maintaining these things, but be aware that they are always a factor. Furthermore, because young men and women on the autism spectrum may also have challenges in communicating their needs, we may need to gently probe for these more basic human needs when they come to us with a problem that looks simply academic. Any coaching that involves improving college readiness must pay attention to each of these factors in addition to the way that a person's diagnosis affects their college readiness.

It is always a good idea to be prepared to look deeper when students' grades start plummeting or their ability to do homework in a timely fashion disappears. Educators are not therapists. It is therefore extremely important that several therapeutic referrals should be available to every coach. Further, those therapists should have experience working with individuals with ASD. Colleges often have their own counseling centers, but not all have experience or knowledge of the effects of ASD on college students. Coaches are better prepared if they get to know a few counselors who have experience or expertise in ASD personally so that they can offer a variety of options to students who show signs of emotional trouble or ignore signs of academic trouble.

Coaching toward competence can assist a student in overcoming executive functioning hurdles such as disorganization and poor time-management skills. The next chapters offers a variety of tools to assist in this area.

Identity

Stage five is often called the "identity crisis." The emerging strength of this stage is known as *fidelity*. Being true to yourself means choosing aspects of the self: to what groups will you belong? What activities will you use to define your "self"? The college campus is full of unique environments and fresh new choices for the average 18- to 22-year-old. It is the perfect laboratory for creating fidelity, but it also can be a tricky place to move around in.

The successful transit of stage five runs through the entire lifetime; however, college seems to be the first time in most people's lives where two things coincide: a huge range of undiscovered choices and consequences are available, and the person has the freedom to explore them without immediate supervision. Our laws and institutions seem to be set up for this. In Western culture, college campuses can often become a relatively safe place for young people to "practice adulthood," make decisions about their daily activities, and work out new and old relationships with an extra element of freedom and responsibility that they did not have while still in grade school. Furthermore, laws like the Family Educational Rights and Privacy Act (FERPA, 1974), though not as restrictive as some assume, essentially protect and shield the privacy of college students by restricting access to their academic records.

The key for any ally is to be able to encourage students to explore these choices while at the same time help the student understand—and, in some cases, preempt—the consequences of the choices that they make. This book later explores how coaching toward fidelity can lead students toward acceptance of their ASD and the ability to self-disclose in ways that are helpful, not harmful.

Intimacy (Affiliational Love)

Students (and parents) usually tell us within the first two meetings we have that they would like to "make friends" or feel more comfortable around people. They hope for themselves (or for their child) that this will happen in college. The appeal can be heart-wrenching, and beyond all other hopes and dreams that allies have for their loved ones, this hope can sometimes seem the least likely to ever come true.

Affiliational love is resolved when a person forms close or intimate relationships (not necessarily sexual) with peers and others and does not succumb to isolation. Coaching can provide a student a broader perspective on social and communication skills, particularly developing and implementing them. This allows them to be aware of the times when mind-blindness, or difficulty seeing events from another's perspective, threatens to throw off their studies. It also may lead to the students finding ways to make friends that are comfortable and that suit their particular needs. Chapter 5 addresses coaching toward this developmental stage.

SUDDEN IMMERSION

When you look back at Eric's first week of college, you could say that it seemed to be a lot less problematic than Sally's. Eric first entered a program that helped him work with the complex effects of his developmental stage and his autism. This launched Eric successfully into college. However, even Eric had some growing to do.

Every transition is a mixed bag, and a transition as large as a person's first week of college is no exception. Preparation can only take a student so far. Getting his or her feet on the ground ahead of time is important, but immersing oneself in college happens rather suddenly and completely. This may be especially true of students who are attending a four-year residential program. I end this chapter with the story of another first week of school and the impact that it had on Mel. Mel is now a professor, and he likes to tell his children and students that it occurred back when "dinosaurs still walked the earth, and no one had ever heard of *autism.*"

TODD

Three years before Mel first encountered the label "autistic," he walked onto his college campus for the first time as a student. The small, Midwestern college he attended was male, and at the time was 70% Greek, as in fraternity. He was one of the few brand new 18-year-old students who did NOT choose to do the fraternity rush. Mel went to two parties but returned very quickly to the dormitory, perplexed and a little terrified at all the structured and somewhat ludicrous social drama that he had witnessed going on in the buildings around campus, whose residents called themselves names like "Tekes," "Fijis," "Lambchops," and "Sigmoids." Upon returning to the dorm, he found three ornate letters each hand drawn on a piece of lined paper and taped crookedly to the door of the building. They were a "G," a "D," and an "I."

Within a day or two, Mel was no longer certain that he had made the right choice of school. College still seemed quite frightening, especially going into musty old rooms with twelve-foot ceilings, stern-faced professors, and classmates who looked either as out-of-place as he felt, or older guys whose demeanor and way of being seemed indecipherable at best and unobtainable at worst. At the height of the freshman's internal anxiety, one of the older guys in the dorm appeared in Mel's open doorway with another student standing somewhat mutely over his left shoulder. He introduced Mel to Todd.

Todd did not talk much, but he smiled freely. He was nearly six feet tall, well over 240 pounds, wore glasses, and walked a little awkwardly. When Todd talked, it was usually at the behest of another student. During their introduction, the other student asked Todd to multiply two different three-digit numbers. This he did in about three seconds with no calculator, paper, or pencil. The only reason this astounding feat took Todd that long was that his speech was very precise and slow. His voice was mellow and he had a southern Indiana accent, but his answers were always correct. The other student handed Mel a calculator and suggested that he race Todd. He did, probably seven or eight times. Todd's answers came out faster than

Mel's fingers could go, and Todd's answers were always correct. The numbers fed to Todd were not rehearsed. Todd was just a slow-talking, strange-walking, heavy-set multiplying machine. Todd and Mel became friends. Todd was the one who finally taught Mel what the three letters on the dorm entrance meant. In his very measured voice, he told him, "It means God *blank* Independent. The 'blank' has six letters, and it starts and ends with a 'D.'"

Years later, Mel came to wonder if Todd was autistic. "When I look back on it now," Mel says, "I realize the irony that a guy as socially awkward as Todd was the first person who made me feel comfortable in my own skin on campus. Because he did, he helped me start to resolve one of the key developmental challenges of my young adult life—Todd became my first college friend."

QUESTIONS

1. What are some of the benefits of using Erikson's developmental theories to discuss college success on the autism spectrum? What are some of the drawbacks?

2. Can you describe a different theory that you believe might work better in this regard?

3. The story about Todd occurred before autism was widely diagnosed. Do you think that Todd was autistic and just not labeled? What evidence do you have that he has succeeded?

4. Do you think that Mel in the Todd story was autistic? What did Mel learn from Todd?

5. What changes might the college they attended consider if they knew this story?

Competence

No More Absent-Minded Professors, or Students

For some reason I have never really understood, the "absent-minded professor" has become an oft-sampled stereotype of academia. Over the years, autistic students I know have bought into this image and even adapted it for themselves. Students with the best view of themselves believe that they are brilliant and unique, and that this combination will get them a college degree. The truth, however, is that it is possible to be "terminally unique"; a certain amount of humility and, yes, *conformity* is required of any person—whether neurotypical or autistic—who obtains a diploma.

An early lesson of young adulthood is that you do not have to have the disheveled look of an Albert Einstein to make a difference in the world. The truly unique aspect of each person arises as he or she takes on the academy's expectations and rises above them one opportunity at a time. Through this process, identity forms against a backdrop of learning and creativity. The truth is that no one obtains a doctorate, or any degree, by being consistently out of touch with the agenda before them, and although everyone who has ever taken a course has also seriously pondered skipping a class, it is never a good idea to avoid those you dislike. Remember Sally...

EXECUTIVE FUNCTIONING
SKILLS AND COMPETENCY

"A foolish consistency is the hobgoblin of little minds, adored by little statesmen and philosophers and divines."

—*EMERSON (1847)*

I first encountered this quote written on the neo-gothic bathroom wall of the Duke University Divinity School Library. I suppose from Socrates to Emerson to that bright-eyed and scraggly haired student who sits in the third row of the Philosophy 101 class, this has been the counter revolutionary anthem of academia, and long may its strain be raised; however, singing that tune will not lead to obtaining a diploma. In addition to talent, knowledge, and diligence, sometimes creating and following a routine is a key element to success.

Young people usually have not had a breadth of experiences or made a great deal of money. However, there is at least one commodity that they are free to save or spend—their time. To be successful all the way to the graduation dais, students must learn to manage their time according to what is required by their university. No matter what their brain wiring, the trick is to make time management as well drilled a skill as anything else they choose to do. Making time for time (management) is key.

On the one hand, this can be good news; students with autism often thrive by following a routine. On the other hand, when cut off from the triggers and regulators of their K–12 school and home environments, the absence of the routine they once counted on can become their biggest hurdle to college success. However, if their coach can help them adapt to the new milieu of college, then their preference for routine can become one of their greatest strengths. To get beyond their own hobgoblins of foolish consistency, students need to perfect their "executive functioning skills."

College success demands this set of competencies (executive functioning skills), including appropriate timing and the ability to summarize and prioritize, and which are often under construction well into late adolescence. Most college freshmen at residential schools struggle with how to structure their evening activities and the demands of their class schedules (for instance, an 8:00 a.m. class is seldom a good idea for a first-year student). Students who come into higher education with autism often report additional timing-specific challenges such as, "I have trouble getting started on things," "I never plan my work in advance," and "I don't have enough time for everything I need to do."

The first assumption to make is that students can become competent in the executive functioning areas of their lives, including time management. We must reject *a priori* the notion that any student is hopelessly "absent-minded." This is more difficult than it sounds. Many students have been convinced—or spent a great deal of energy convincing others—that they will never make it to an appointment on time or be able to focus on a task at hand. The job of a good coach is to replace this notion with the idea that every adult uses tools, techniques, and strategies to stay on top of his or her life.

Many different tools are available to people to organize their time; in fact, entire companies have made millions off this need. Numerous apps do it electronically; however, in order to manage the task of teaching time management to an entire cohort of students within the first semester of college, it is wise for coaches to use a specific tool for the entire group. The system offered in the following discussion works in conjunction with the syllabi the students receive for each class, and the program and institution's calendar. That way the coach can more easily monitor all the students he or she is supporting, and the students may be able to help each other with time management under the right circumstances.

SHOW ME, DON'T TELL ME

One of the most complicated challenges that can occur during a coaching session is for the student with autism to say, "I've got my schedule in my head." This may be true—certainly, the student believes it. However, knowing *what* you need to study and *how* you will make that happen is just as vital as the accuracy of the information in your head. Some students pride themselves on their ability to remember data, including the dates and times for various appointments, but too often situations arise that can make follow-up difficult or impossible, especially during the first year of college. Thus, it is important for coach and student to teach and learn a mutually agreed-upon system of scheduling to ensure that circumstances do not trump the very best of intentions.

Any system that will be helpful for executive functioning challenges should have these basic components:

- Thorough and well defined
- Visual
- Flexible
- Electronically adaptable

To be thorough, define all the items put onto the schedule block. Schedules are made up of time blocks, and the average collegian's schedule includes many different kinds of time. For instance, there is dead time, meaning short periods between classes with nothing scheduled. There is free time, which is essential and can include breaks, workouts, lunch, or just sitting and thinking. There is even reward time, which is contingent on accomplishing the goals set out for the week. When students buy into the idea of rewarding themselves with something fun after all the work is finished, reward time can prove to be the strongest motivator to get a person through the week. However, it is very helpful to remind students that free time is different from reward time. You can see examples of each of these kinds of time in the sample schedule block that follows.

Alas, work does have to come first, and a study schedule is primarily about, well, studying. Two things clarify what "studying" means. First, studying is not an amorphous activity. It consists of several different specific activities (see "Kinds of Time/Prioritizing" in the Appendix). Studying includes undertakings as wide and varied as reading, memorizing, or writing. Each of these activities can be even more specific: I am not simply reading from 10:00 to 11:00, but I am *reading chapter 2 in the history textbook*; I am not writing my paper, but I am *putting together the outline for the first half of the assignment*. Coaches and allies can encourage students to provide details when they say "I'm studying," but regardless, schedules should follow this rule of thumb: *at least two hours of studying outside of class for every one hour in class.* Because many studies indicate that visual cues are important to students with Asperger's syndrome or autism, in order to help students see if they are following this guideline, the schedule suggested here can be color-coded or icon-coded.

The students assign a color, or visual icon, to each class they are taking—for instance, English 101 may be red (paper) and Math

101 blue (pi symbol). In the sample study block, the student first puts the class lecture and lab hours for her math class on the schedule with a corresponding pi symbol. Then she adds in study time for the same class and inserts the same symbol in these time blocks. Visually, it then becomes a simple matter of seeing whether the five classroom hours of Math 101 per week also includes ten hours of corresponding study time, also highlighted with a pi symbol. If it does not, then make adjustments before the coach agrees to the schedule.

Students complete the schedule on a weekly basis, but it also has to be flexible. There needs to be room to add any appointments that arise to the chart, including nonacademic activities such as clubs, workout time, meal times, and even free time. It is important for students to buy into the structure of the schedule. Sometimes students are able to adapt to the new schedule so thoroughly that they have difficulty straying from it even if circumstances change. More often, the students have trouble, at least initially, putting forth the effort needed to comply with the schedules they set for themselves. Either way, the most successful students eventually adapt to using the scheduling procedure on a regular, weekly basis. Support them to make sure they work dead time, free time, class time, lab time, study time, and reward time into the schedule. For a sample schedule block, see Appendix.

In the sample schedule block (Fig. 3.1) on the following page, please notice that the student maintains two-to-one rule of thumb. Appointments have a yellow (checkmark); free time is labeled with a happy face (white); reward time has a star (light orange). The student goes to a nonresidential school and thus is only on campus from 8:00 a.m. to 3:00 p.m.

- English 101 = red or 📄

- Math 101 = blue or π

- Appointments = yellow or ☑

- Free time = white or ☺

- Reward time = light orange or ★

FIG. 3.1 WEEK OF: September 22–28

	Monday	Tuesday	Wednesday	Thursday	Friday
8:00	Coffee ☺	Coffee ☺	Coffee with Sandy ☺	Write response 🗋	Complete draft 🗋
9:00	Read pp. 89–99 🗋	Section 1.3 Problems 1–10 in textbook π	Go to Math tutoring room π	Review notes π	Finish problems π
10:00	Math 101 class π	Math 101 class π	Math 101 class π	Math 101 lab π	Math 101 class QUIZ 2 π
11:00	1:1 with academic coach ☑	Section 1.4 Problems 3–33 Lunch π	Section 1.6 Problems 3–8 π	Study for quiz—do review problem π	Section 1.8 Problems 5–54 Lunch π
12:00	Fitness center Lunch ☺	English 101 🗋	English 101 🗋	Fitness center Lunch ☺	English 101 🗋
1:00	Sign-up for Math Tutoring ☑	Drop in to see Professor S. after class to look at syllabus 🗋	Lunch ☺	Take Essay 1 to Writing Center 🗋	Aspy group ☑
2:00	Sections 1.2–1.3 π	Write response to 89–99 🗋	Read pp. 99–108 🗋	Writing Center 🗋	REWARD: ★ Play video games into the night…

A blank copy of this schedule is available in the Appendix. There is also another version of the schedule block that shows how the student can map out his or her time to meet the two-to-one ratio of study time to class time using numbered blocking.

In the end, the most important thing is to make time for creating a schedule each week and finding the support to make this balanced and realistic. Because autistics, by definition, can often have problems being flexible, the second most important thing to do is learn that sometimes even a well-designed schedule has to be adapted. Work is not always done in the time allotted, and sometimes someone cannot make an appointment. Sometimes work is done early. Regular coaching support is essential when changes cause anxiety or stress in a student. With time, students eventually learn to work through change better if they have a schedule and are doing their best to follow it.

For the first half of the transition year, the student should meet with the coach twice a week. Much of the first meeting time is used for creating the scheduling block because that is where everything comes together; students bring their syllabi and course calendar. The student notes dates and assignments on the schedule, the coach holds a discussion about what needs done that week, and the student and coach create schedules for the coming week. At the end of the week, students check in to see how well they followed their schedules and what they might change to make them easier to follow the next week. These schedules are stored and sent electronically, and students are encouraged to attach alarms and warnings to them if they want. They also receive a printout of it to carry around. In short, their schedules should be in front of them as often as possible in order to encourage their use and refinement. Zoe Gross wrote an interesting essay related to this topic, "Better Living through Prosthetic Brain Parts."

By the second semester, students may choose to keep this scheduling system, tweak it, or dump it in favor of another system. All changes have to be thoroughly discussed with the coach, but the idea of the schedule block is to develop an effective technique, not tie someone down to just one method of time management and organization for their entire college career. At its best, the schedule becomes both a visual structure to rely on, and a way of illustrating how to manage change—managing change is really the ultimate goal because long after the students' first semester in college, they will still experience change in their lives.

In many ways, stage four is only successfully resolved when people learn to adapt to new environments and expectations in ways that no longer make them feel inferior or out of touch. Many students with autism suffer from others' perception that they are "lazy" or "incompetent" if they are not able to meet deadlines immediately in the new college environment. However, by learning to adapt and modify a tool like the schedule block to their needs and the demands of their academic institutions, we can avoid the brand "absent-minded."

WHAT ABOUT AN "ABSENT-MINDED" PROFESSOR?

Creating and following a time schedule depends on being able to easily ascertain what the assignments and due dates are. When instructors do not have a clear set of written expectations, it cripples every student's ability to grow in competency. At its worst, a disorganized class becomes a case of "guess what the professor is thinking" when it comes to assignments and expectations. Such guessing is a challenge for all students, but it can be especially incapacitating for students on the spectrum who may have difficulty understanding the simplest elements of another person's viewpoint precisely because of their diagnosis. The disorganized professor is becoming more and more of an anachronism in modern education as tracking and curriculum systems like Blackboard become part of the higher education tool set; however, it is still possible to run into teachers whose style does not gel with the autistic mind.

There is only a limited number of things that a student can do when this happens. One, they can do their best to cope with the disorganization with the help of fellow students and regular student–instructor meetings. Two, the student can create their own organizing system (Fig. 3.2) to track the grades and assignments in the class like one created by a student that is available in the Appendix.

FIG. 3.2 Example Student Assignment Record

ENG 251			
Assignment	Due date	%	Grade
Essay 1	4/26	25%	25/25
Essay 2	5/12	25%	25/25
Essay 3		25%	20/25
Quizzes		25%	

Three, the student can notice the problem as early as possible in the semester and drop the disorganized professor in favor of a different class or an alternative section with a different instructor.

UNEVEN KNOWLEDGE SCHEMA: HONORING SPECIAL INTERESTS

Effective time-management tools are one way of helping a student adapt their competency challenges to the college environment. Another essential component of stage four is the degree to which a student has confidence and a history of accomplishment in some area of knowledge. Many students have found particular areas in which they are competent, even exceptional, by the time they walk onto campus, and competency in these areas can become the basis for competency in general.

For students with autism, most people refer to these areas as "special interests," although many autistics object to this term. Another way of thinking about this aspect of autism is as an uneven knowledge schema. It is possible to be an expert in one subject but know very little about another. When a person has both an expertise and a high degree of fascination in just one area of knowledge, they can lose sight of the importance of other ideas or topics.

In the case of autism, uneven knowledge schemas can range from encyclopedic knowledge of science, video games, or sports to particular affinities for solving math problems, creating art, or performing music. Many autistics are rewarded or even celebrated in these areas; however, most autistics have also experienced the "zone-out" that crosses other people's faces when they get too stuck on their special interest in the wrong social setting. Having competency in an area and *feeling* like a competent person is not always the same thing. Furthermore, not all the areas in which a student is competent will help him or her succeed in college (or in life).

The "How Will I Know If I'm Ready for College?" Exercise

One way to maintain respect for the competencies that autistics have and build off them is to use the "How Will I Know If I'm Ready for College?" exercise (see Appendix on page 194). In this activity, the coach presents students one column at a time, of a three-column table.

When presenting the student with the first column, ask them to list "What I'm Good At." This has been known to include things like "doodles," "walking," "anything to do with the Civil War," games such as *Super Mario Bros.* or *Left 4 Dead*; "making friends"; and "taking care of pets." The point of column one is for the students to name, and be proud of, their interests and competencies.

Next, the students fill in the second column, a list of what they think they will be good at in college. Interesting discussions arise from this step. For instance, this column is presented to the students and they are encouraged to imagine themselves in the new setting and make a list of "what I expect to be good at in college." Their expectations about how they will do in that new setting are often skewed either to the overconfident side, or to the "deer in the headlights, I just don't know" side. In our program, the students do this exercise during an extended orientation week prior to classes, so they have seen the buildings and experienced the campus a little, but with no other students and no classes yet on their radar. This list is often, understandably, shorter. It may include the same or similar things as the first column, but occasionally a student can also be understood as stretching their expectations, or even naming their hopes: "navigating around campus," "self-control," "reading," and "finding friends" are a few of the items seen on these lists.

Finally, move to Column C. Students with autism who are now upperclassmen completed this list. Its heading is "what I'm expected to be good at in college." The items on this list grow and change each year, because they come from students on the spectrum who have already completed their first year. They have listed several practical things that incoming students may have experienced, such as "talking to other students in order to make friends" and many things that incoming students may not yet have even considered, such as "talking to other students about classes" and "working in groups." They also include items that incoming students may have listed in columns A and B, such as "finding classrooms, faculty offices, facilities, and departments," and items that are much more complex, such as "knowing what my learning style is, and telling instructors." Mostly, the column C list leans toward the very practical, including items having to do with buying books, getting into programs of study, and knowing where the writing lab and/or math learning center is on campus.

The final step in the exercise serves as a reality check for the students. In it, students compare the three sets of columns and write down "misses" and "matches." For students who are not very facile at verbal communication, the comparison displays many things; for students who love to talk, the graph provides some structure for their commentary. The point is to ease the student from a self-defined understanding of being good at something to an understanding of the things they may need to get better at in order to succeed in the college setting.

A comparison of columns B and C lets the student know that college is more than they imagined it to be. By reminding the incoming students that the C items come from students just like them who have made it through this new jungle of expectations, you bolster their confidence.

Unlike neurotypical students, this connection sometimes has to be "engineered" for autistics. Thoughtful coaching finds ways to bring former and first-time students into dialogue and then step out of the way. A coach can do this through formal structures, such as the TRIO program or various mentoring programs, on a college campus, or in other, less formal ways.

For instance, one student on the spectrum obtained a work-study job in his college admissions department during his second year of school. Below is the text from a PowerPoint presentation he created. He regularly presents this to a small group of incoming freshman, some of whom are autistic, some of whom are not.

1. DO your assignments on time
2. DO check out the fun things on campus
3. DO get your disability forms in to your professors
4. DO meet new people on campus
5. DO ask for help
6. DO check your email and Blackboard
7. DO use the writing center
8. DO form a bond with one of your professors
9. DO find a hangout
10. DO enjoy your time in college

1. DO NOT leave your email unattended
2. DO NOT ignore any problems you may have
3. DO NOT give up!
4. DO NOT forget your campus ID at home
5. DO NOT stress too much
6. DO NOT forget to study
7. DO NOT be afraid to go exploring on campus

8. DO NOT wait to check your Blackboard grades until it's too late

9. DO NOT be nervous about trying new activities

10. DO NOT think you're not fit for college

BONUS: DO NOT ask the school mascot out. She's mine!

Finally, because no one really likes forcing someone into a reality check, it is essential that any exercise end with the coach or teacher reiterating to the new student that they have fantastic and interesting competencies and interests. There should be more than just the taste of "if they did it, then you can do it" in the incoming student's mouth when the exercise is over. There should be a solid understanding of what skills they have for college already and what interests they have that might help them obtain a particular major like history or video game design. It should help them work on the expectations the college has for them as the coming year looms. To this final point, the incoming student should also feel secure that the coach is there for them as they set out.

Executive functioning deficits can be addressed in numerous ways, but until an autistic student has confidence in the skills they possess and is able to see that those competencies and interests have some relevance to academia, the workaday of making it to appointments on time and breaking up big assignments into smaller units is unlikely to motivate them.

THE PRINCIPLE OF FADING SUPPORT

No matter how a coach addresses competency issues, the principle of fading support is essential. Coaches may need to be the clocks and checklists for their students at first. They may need to continue this support for quite some time, but their interventions should always keep an exit strategy in mind. Just when and how to back off from dependency is an art as well as a science. For example, here is a list of possible interventions for teaching timing skills in descending order:

- Assign student time and tasks
- Keep student calendar in the coach's office
- Give a list of time and tasks from which the student chooses
- Use electronic reminders

As I mentioned before, students are ultimately responsible for choosing their own scheduling style and technology. For some, simple notes in a pocket calendar work; for others, fancy phone apps or elaborate "Day Runner"-type systems are best. Coaches and allies introduce these things, but students have to intentionally choose and use them. Students also can be encouraged to find friends, roommates, or electronic ways to be reminded how, when, and where to get things done.

 ## KALEEL KNEELS

Each student is a unique individual with a distinctive set of skills and competencies, only some of which come from the effects of autism. Others do not. As a result, remember that some people, including autistics, actually have a strong competency in timing skills. For instance, Kaleel kept a nearly perfect internal clock and calendar. If anyone wanted to know what day of the week July 19, 2021, would fall on, he could tell him or her instantly. If a faculty person was five minutes late back to her office for Kaleel's one o'clock appointment, she would get a lecture from him, and deservedly so! He was brilliant at timing, far better than most people will ever be. Most people got used to this trait, but he had another trait that often disturbed others.

Kaleel spoke to himself on a regular basis. His words were very quiet, and even though they were hard to make out, a listener could tell they were rhythmical. At first, most people ignored his subtonic speech, but one day during a particularly intense one-on-one session, the coach found it just too annoying and abruptly asked him to stop. Kaleel refused.

After a couple of weeks, the behavior did not abate. Every week during the scheduled hour, Kaleel would shift to self-talk, so the coach decided to pay more attention to it and see if he could figure out what it meant. One day, quite unplanned, Kaleel began telling his coach about the dance he had gone to the weekend before at his mosque. The next time he began what others had labeled "self-talk," the coach realized what was really going on, and he changed his meeting time with Kaleel.

Who better than Kaleel to know the exact times for pausing in the midst of the busy school day to quietly recite one's daily prayers?

 QUESTIONS

1. What is your understanding of the archetype called "the absent-minded professor"? Do you feel that it is an accurate representation of a certain kind of personality? Who have you known (or do you consider yourself) to fit this archetype? Can we change this?

2. What are the basic competencies that you feel people need to have in order to succeed in college? If you are in a mixed group, divide into staff/faculty and students, each group make a list, and then compare them.

3. What are the advantages or disadvantages of spending time organizing time? Is the schedule block from this chapter something you could see yourself adapting? Would it work for others you know? What other ways do people organize their classes, homework, and lives that you have found to be helpful?

4. Try the "How will I know if I'm ready for college?" exercise and discuss the results.

5. What are your "Do and Do Not" lists? How might they differ from the ones presented in this chapter? How might they be the same?

6. Do you agree with the principle of fading support? How fast or slow do you think it should begin once implemented? Are there other areas (besides time and scheduling) where you feel that a college student could use some fading support?

7. Name some unique competencies (like Kaleel's awareness of time) that you have. How have they helped you take on the challenges of higher education—whether you are a freshman or a tenured professor—over the years?

Identity

Making an Entrance

C onsider how true the bumper sticker is that says, "My Kid and My Money Go to XYZ University." In an article on its website, the National Retail Federation said that in 2012, back-to-school and back-to-college spending would total about $83.8 billion (Little). Although that figure took in many forms of merchandise, a sizable chunk probably went to the purchase of college and university-stamped mugs, flags, notebooks, and especially apparel. Why do students and their families buy so many "XYZ University" and "ABC State" items?

COLUMBUS STATE
COMMUNITY COLLEGE

I think that one reason is it helps resolve the "identity vs. role confusion" stage. When someone is wearing an "ABC State" shirt, everyone knows where he or she belongs. It is a great way to demonstrate where allegiance lies and what priorities are playing out in the wearer's life. There is no way to doubt that a sense of identity and even comfort can come from such self-labeling. For instance, because I live near OSU (*Ohio State University*, not that other one in Oklahoma), it is extremely common to see university branding while walking all over town and to feel bonded to it. When I see the university's logo in another state—such as at an airport or even on a beach—an automatic (albeit illusory) kinship develops between the person in the OSU shirt and myself. The best part is, I don't even teach at OSU, nor have I ever been a student there!

For a young adult student who finds him- or herself transported onto a new, unknown, and maybe even frightening campus environment—wearing an "XYZ University" shirt or hat often eases the uncertainty and makes them feel accepted and involved.

Furthermore, a great deal of commitment and single-minded effort is involved in the process of preparing for college, choosing a college, and starting college on the right foot. This is true not only for the students, but also for their family members, especially if the student is on the spectrum. The greater the effort required to get on the road to higher education, the greater the sense of identity that may come from the result, and the greater the identification a student has with an institution of higher education, the greater the loyalty that comes along with it.

So hear ye, hear ye, boards of directors! Help first-generation and autistic students succeed, and you will have strong alumni for life.

With all this in mind, it is no wonder that a student's first on-campus introduction to college often includes a trip to the apparel section of the bookstore.

THE ADMISSIONS INTERVIEW
"College is Different? I Don't Like *Different*"

An admissions counselor recounted the following story:

> Wade first came into my office in the admissions department a full 3 months before his matriculation date. He was carrying a large, full bag with the college bookstore logo on it. When he sat down, Wade was practically hidden behind the huge sack, which he placed on his lap between himself and me.
>
> It is my job to greet new students and get them enthused about coming to my school. I did not need to enthuse Wade. He began talking about our school from the first word out of his mouth. He

was already wearing the brand new polo shirt with the college logo on it that he had just bought. He was ready for the ball games and the dining hall (where he had just been to lunch with his older sister); however, as we talked, I wasn't sure how ready Wade was for the classes, so I began by telling him how the expectations for students are different in college than they were in high school.

By the end of our interview, the cheery Wade who had just come bouncing through my door looked deflated. Internally, I began to wonder what I had done. My career rather depends on students leaving my office more fired up about coming to my school than they were when they walked in—not less. Did I give Wade too much reality too fast? Apparently, that was the cause of Wade's disconsolation, because as he left, he said to me, "College is different? I don't like different."

A first-year college student has to deal with two kinds of difference in college. On the one hand, college is simply a different environment from high school, with very dissimilar expectations. In K–12, school personnel are tasked with providing a "free and appropriate public education" in the "least-restrictive environment." In higher education, the personnel only need to provide accommodations that assure equal access. This means that it becomes incumbent on a young adult student to ask for accommodations and support. Parents, allies, and professionals cannot do this for the student. This radical shift happens the moment a student is accepted into a higher education program.

On the other hand, college is often also quite different from the expectations we have of it. Autistics are often excellent at setting up and following routines, and understanding the patterns they find out in the world. The shift from high school to college always comes with a need to shift routines and understand the new patterns that come with adulthood and higher education. Making this shift does not need to restrict new college students, but it requires them to focus on becoming flexible and adaptable in ways that are likely to push them out of their comfort zones.

CLAIMING AUTISM AS PART OF IDENTITY

Before people can be realistic about what their academic strengths and challenges are, they must first be able to accept all aspects of their psyche. This is a lifelong task and adventure, but at eighteen or nineteen years of age, the journey begins in earnest. For many people, accepting and understanding what autism is and how it affects their lives is difficult, but it is also crucial if they are to hone their ability to self-disclose in ways that are helpful, not harmful.

Most students receive their autism diagnosis these days at some point in their childhood, long before they have the capacity to understand what it is. They have sat through dozens of IEP and other school support meetings by the time they arrive on campus, but often they have never really taken part in the meetings as a full and viable adult participant. Frequently when asked the question, "What is autism?" first-year students find this difficult to answer. When they were children, they needed a parent or other adult to speak on their behalf; however, now it is essential to claim autism as part of their makeup, and be conversant in what it is and how it affects them. This is difficult to do intellectually and emotionally. It requires maturity and willingness on the part of the student on the spectrum to study the diagnosis and all of the implications it has on his or her life.

Many people with autism have an understandable attitude that sounds something like this: "What good is a diagnosis when I am really not 'disabled'? I can figure out how to go to college without a diagnosis, lots of people do." Therefore, they come to college and do not seek support, and to some extent, it makes sense. Students who had an autism label in grade school, for instance, may come to feel that shedding it completely and starting over with a clean slate in college is a refreshing alternative they want for themselves. College is a time of transition where "all the planets align" for a person to make different kinds of decisions, even when others disagree with them.

As Ari Ne'eman (2013) wrote in the foreword to *Navigating College: A Handbook on Self-Advocacy Written for Autistic Students from Autistic Adults*:

> One of the most important realizations you can make as you become an adult is that there is nothing wrong with making decisions that others disagree with. Our family members are frequently our strongest allies—but part of growing up is making choices, even and especially those that are different from the choices that other people would make for us. (viii)

A college-age person understandably wishes to make his or her own decisions—and choosing to take on college without a diagnosis around the neck is a clear and independent choice. It seems logical; after all, a diagnosis is just a name given to a set of characteristics.

I encourage students with this belief to expand their perspective a little. Perhaps it is not just, "What good is a diagnosis?" but instead can be, "What good might I do with what a diagnosis says about me?" Balking against a label is admirable up to a point, but can become self-defeating.

The real problem with a diagnosis, or any other kind of label, happens when the label takes the place of the full and complete person. On the other hand, it is possible to accept a diagnosis and not let it completely define who you are (Williams, 2005). Furthermore, by rejecting all diagnoses outright, we end up claiming our own individual identity at the expense of downplaying the amazing intellectual diversity found in the human population.

What part of autism is disability and what part is diversity? This debate is where personal transformation begins.

DIVERSITY AND DISABILITY

Working in the field of autism studies, relative strangers sometimes ask me, "Have you ever been diagnosed with autism?" My reply is, "I have to wear glasses." Autism is a diagnosis, and a diagnosis is primarily a description.

There are several things to bear in mind about a diagnosis. First, autism is traditionally considered a syndrome—that is, a collection of symptoms. Therefore, whether in the title of Leo Kanner's 1943 article, "Autistic Disturbances of Affective Contact," or in the DSM-5 criteria (American Psychiatric Association), "autism" *describes*—it never *prescribes*. One should never assume that because a description of a person contains the word *autistic*, he or she should therefore be—or do—anything. Autism is *not* a curable disease, and one cannot take any pill or powder to get rid of it.

Second, because autism does not prescribe, it should never proscribe anyone from pursuing goals. Everyone is full of potential energies that will propel a person to learn or become many, many things. Autism helps you narrow the field (as does having to wear glasses), but it is a diagnosis, and that is never a *complete* definition of anyone. The truth about every diagnosis is that people can have the same thing and be different from each other more than they are similar. Diversity, not disability, is the more important definition.

Since the Civil Rights Movement, we have defined *diversity* in racial, ethnic, and cultural terms, and acceptance of the concept of diversity has led to new fields of study in academia including black studies and women's studies. Beginning in the 2000s, the term "neurodiversity" began to emerge among those in the autistic community. Most neurotypical people are not yet familiar with the movement. However, writers such as Steve Silberman are starting to define neurodiversity as "the notion that conditions like autism, dyslexia, and attention-deficit/hyperactivity disorder (ADHD) should be regarded as naturally occurring cognitive variations with distinctive strengths that have contributed to the evolution of technology and culture rather than mere checklists of deficits and dysfunctions," (2015, p. 16). In his book, *NeuroTribes: The Legacy of Autism and the Future of Neurodiversity*, Silberman stresses, through his extensive research into the history of Leo Kanner, Hans Asperger, and other major characters in autism history, that neurodiversity is not a new idea. Instead, it has been present since the earliest work of Hans Asperger in the 1930s and 1940s.

Silberman explains that the first two progenitors of the autism diagnosis, Kanner and Asperger, differed in their view of whom the autism diagnosis included. For Kanner, autism was a narrowly-defined childhood psychiatric illness. He was very proud of the number of children he turned away *without* a diagnosis of autism because their conditions were not severe enough. Asperger, on the other hand, proposed the idea that autism was a commonplace form of cognition shared by many people, even in 1938, decades before the term "neurodiversity" first entered the public lexicon. In fact, Asperger and his colleagues thought of the "little professors" they worked with as members of varying tribes, and they thought of their work as helping them find jobs and careers that suited their unique capacities best.

When Uta Frith published her report in 1991 on Asperger and his clinic, it led her to propose the idea of the autism spectrum. This concept places all of us on psychology's all-purpose "tool" de force: the "bell" curve. Some of us, according to this characterization, have few autistic characteristics and are thus on the left side of the curve. Others have many autistic characteristics, placing us on on the right side of the curve. Most of us languish in the middle, or "normal" section of the curve—not too hot and not too cold. The curve of the autism spectrum ultimately allows families and individuals with the diagnosis to become more "acceptable" in the neurotypical culture that surrounds them (still a work in progress). Still, it reduces the understanding of autism; the individual and his or her autistic traits fall on a specific point somewhere on a two-dimensional line drawing like the one below.

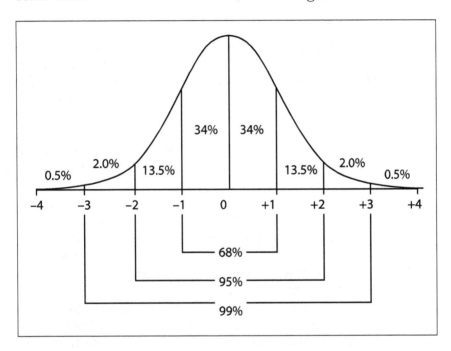

As an alternative visual to the bell curve, I offer you ... marbles. I must confess that marbles are a wonder to me. I can go on all day about the history, beauty, worth, and value of them, but what makes them most relevant as a teaching tool is that they expand and concretize how we have defined autism up until now.

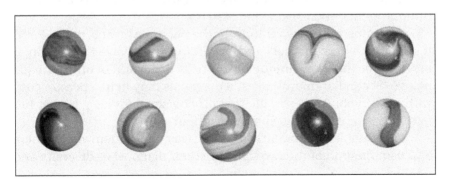

Look at the ten marbles in the picture. What makes them different? How are they beautiful? How are they valuable? How valuable do you think they are? Would you like to hold them in your hand? Look at them under a light? A black light? A magnifying glass? Or would you just appreciate them as they are without special equipment?

Now, how are the ten marbles the same?

If you look closely, you will see that all ten marbles have a particular color in them. It is a deep iron red color called "oxblood." Do you see it? These marbles are a hundred-plus years old, and it is my understanding that modern artisans have never duplicated the oxblood color in them.

This is what autism in a person looks like. Some have a lot of it. Some have barely a speck. For some students, their autism swirls and swells. For others, it forms a thin line throughout their whole being. All people, of course, are more than their autism—they are more than deep red, they are blue or green, and maybe yellow or gold, white or egg yolk cream. The marble exercise reminds allies, coaches, professors, teachers, parents, children, siblings, lovers, counselors, politicians, pastors, and higher education professionals that we are much more than our diagnosis, much more complex than the point we occupy on a bell curve.

For the purposes of this book, the emerging concept of neurodiversity describes autism as one kind of naturally-occurring difference found in the human species. We can attribute the autistic form of neurodiversity to observable and measurable neurological differences in human brain chemistry and function. Peter Vermeulen sums this up succinctly, "The behavior and choices a person makes do impact their success and happiness in the world. However, the behaviors associated with autism are not autism; instead, the behaviors are the effect of autism. Autism is about the brain. It is not about behavior," (2014).

A diagnosis does two things for the person who accepts it. First, it supports a person's self-understanding and allows the person to begin to see just how unique he or she is in a world of other unique beings. Second, in many cases, a diagnosis may help a person cope with certain challenges in life that otherwise might keep him or her from joy, success, and self-actualization.

It is possible for students to see the way that autism affects them as a combination of the two halves of their diagnosis—diversity and disability. It is important to help students start thinking about accepting autism as both a form of human diversity and a starting point from which to get needs met so that they do not altogether reject the information their diagnosis may give them or feel "less than" because of the diagnosis. In other words, "autism" is a label, but labels in and of themselves do not always have to be avoided or shunned. They can be an especially useful starting point from which young people begin to define who they are as they step into a college setting.

Diversity and Disability Exercise (Marbles)

Use marbles in this exercise. They are a good choice because they vary by color, pattern, size, age, and feel; however, really any class of collectible could be substituted as long as the facilitator has an expertise and a passion that he or she can translate to the students.

One common teaching technique in K–12 is called "power cards." A coach uses the strong interests that elementary age students have in, for example, Pokémon, as a springboard to introduce other subjects. Instead of using marbles, a coach might learn what strong interests his or her college students have that are age-appropriate for this exercise, and use them.

Participants begin by choosing four of the marbles or other collectibles and describing them on paper—they can even draw them out. While they are describing the pieces, they are taught the categories that define sets of the collectibles (in the case of marbles, the names of the marbles, like "German Swirl," "China Clay," and "Latticinio Core;" information on marbles can be found on websites such as Block's Marble Auction). Once they are done describing the items they have, participants are asked to categorize each collectible they described and put it on the chart. They then talk about how the item is useful or used, and finally, estimate what they feel the collectible item is worth—how much they would pay for it, and why?

Describe the collectible	Categorize it	How is it useful or used	Give it a value

Once the chart is completed, the participants discuss the following points:

1. How unique is each item that you described or drew? What makes each item different? What makes them the same?
2. Do you agree with the way the collectibles are categorized by others? Which is your favorite category, least favorite category?
3. What words did you use when you described the use or usefulness of each item? Why did you choose those words?
4. What informed the value you gave to each collectible the most—its beauty, history, rarity, investment potential, something else?

Hand out a variety of collectibles to keep the discussion lively. They should vary according to age, pattern, method of manufacture, and rarity. Hand out noticeably broken collectibles, and collectibles that would not be considered very valuable by an auctioneer or dealer.

Discussions following this exercise often get participants to start thinking about the possible connections between the ability to "do" something and the inherent value of anything that "does." This, in turn, often leads to deeper discoveries about just what "value" is, and how people determine it. Finally, the lesson hinges on expanding the metaphors of usefulness and value to the way we perceive concepts like ability and disability, value, and human worth.

The exercise works best when the students and participants can relate to collecting the items, but are not expert collectors themselves. If they are, the discussion can quickly get derailed because some participants may have difficulty getting beyond the concrete thinking involved in the first steps and into the symbolic thinking involved in the discussion afterward (see question 3 at the end of the chapter). To counter this, the skilled facilitator can come equipped with plenty of examples of human diversity, and the way human disability is formally and informally defined and understood. The last step asks the participants to extend the lesson by applying it to their own understanding of how autism affects them personally. You can even give each participant his or her own collectible item to remind them of the lesson. At this point, some participants may still balk at the idea of applying the autism label, whereas others may find relief from the oppressive feelings that arise from having a label.

SELF-DISCLOSURE

Others are usually the ones who label, and it often hurts those on the receiving end. Sometimes, however, a person may find value in labeling him- or herself. When one does this in a public space, or with a staff person or peer, we call it "self-disclosure." Self-disclosure is the main reason why it is important to consolidate identity, because knowing who you are allows you to ask others for support in ways that get results. Self-disclosure involves a complex set of social skills. Consider all the aspects of telling someone (usually a stranger to you until then) about how autism affects you. People who self-disclose effectively are able to:

- Accept that they are on the spectrum.
- Know how being autistic affects them.
- Verbalize or write the effects out in ways that others can appreciate and understand.
- Read a situation and determine if it is the correct time, person, and place to share.
- Know if the person or persons with whom they are sharing are trustworthy.
- Maintain the balance between telling nothing and telling everything.
- Know what kinds of support to ask for and whether this person can provide it.
- Know why they are self-disclosing—what they expect as a result, and what happens if they do not meet that expectation.

A teaching technique known as "social narratives" used with younger students may be adapted for guiding students through the self-disclosure process. Even jokes can work: "A young man was speeding through a small town when he was pulled over by the local sheriff. When the officer appeared at his window, the young man said, 'I know I was going 45 in a 25 zone. I was texting my mom, but I did see the speed limit sign.' The officer said, 'Thanks for all that information, son, but I just pulled you over to tell you your taillight is out.'"

Coaches and allies can go a long way toward laying this all out systematically, and peers may be the best persons to provide feedback on whether they see the autistic's self-disclosure technique is working. Consider this illustration:

> My friend Veronica raised her hand today five minutes into our biology class and began to explain what "autism" is, apropos of nothing—the lecture was on diabetes. She and I had talked for hours last Saturday night at the Student Union about how autism affects her; I had learned a lot from her and been impressed by her understanding of it and her willingness to ask me for support. I really did not know what to do when I saw the other students squirming in their chairs. I am concerned that she is going to have problems in school unless she figures out a way to reign herself in.

Veronica had only recently started to read up on her diagnosis and become involved with the broader autism culture and community. To her, there was no more important topic than those that had to do with autism. Ironically, she would later come to learn that it was partially because of her autism that she was becoming hyper-focused on autism. Because she had trouble reading other people's reactions, she did not always know when to "pass on a chance to educate others about autism," as she would say. Luckily, Veronica had a loving friend who pointed this out to her. After another Saturday night session, Veronica and her friend went to the biology professor's office and asked if they could share the topic, "Biological Differences in Autistic Cognition," for their paired semester project. The professor agreed, and they both earned an A, thanks in part to Veronica's personal passion for the subject.

College students are discovering whom they are and with whom they wish to identify. Student centers, clubs, and activities based on self-identifiers such as gender, culture, interest, or race often thrive on a college campus precisely because they assist young people with the developmental task known as identity vs. role confusion. Working together as friends and associates who support the expression and exploration of all differences, including intellectual differences, in positive ways is life-enriching for students with autism, their allies and friends, and the institutions they attend.

In whatever way you approach the topic of identity and autism, the ultimate goal is for a student to claim that they are a person with brain wiring that is different from the brain wiring of others they might encounter. Furthermore, it is essential to accept that this difference can lead to challenges in the college environment. Such a claim does not have to lead to shame or failure; in fact, if taken in the spirit of joy and acceptance, it can lead to some funny experiences.

 ## I'M AN AUTISTIC KID WHEN I'M AT DISNEYLAND

Byron found himself on the horns of a dilemma one spring break in Florida. Over the years, he had learned to control his anxiety when it came to crowds; in fact, he had learned a lot about how autism affected him in general. There was a moment while at Disneyland that spring, however, that it all came back. The line to a ride was mega-long and full of the noise of "human chatter-birds" and the smells of suntan oil and sweat. All the overstimulation threatened to send him into a meltdown, though it had been years since he last had one. He worried about embarrassing himself and his housemates; it had all been so great until then.

Out of the corner of his eye, he saw a young girl and her mom escorted to the front of the line. The daughter wore leg braces and used two walking sticks. Byron smiled and called his friends over into a huddle.

"Did you guys notice that there is a policy for bringing handicapped kids to the front of the line?" After the other three acknowledged that they did, Byron went on. "OK, so I am going to go *Rain Man* on 'em here in a minute. One of you go get the docent and tell her that your 'brother' has autism. Ask real politely if she can bring me and the rest of you to the front of the line, OK?"

According to his own telling of the story, Byron switched it on and got a double reward. First, he got a little relief from the built-up anxiety. Second, he and his "brothers" got to the front of the line, fast. He has repeated this strategy several times since when he finds himself in similar situations—with a wink.

QUESTIONS

1. What's your favorite college-branded item? If it is apparel, talk about why you bought it and/or how you feel when you wear it. Is it a stretch to say that wearing an "ABC State" or "XYZ University" T-shirt helps resolve the identity vs. role confusion stage of development? Why or why not?

2. What do you suppose were Wade's expectations of how college would be different from high school? Whether student, faculty, or staff, how have your expectations of your higher education institution changed? When you introduce yourself in an off-campus setting, how long does it take you to mention the name of your college and your connection to it?

3. Stand up and line up on the floor. As the following statements from this chapter are read, move forward to the degree that you agree with each statement or move backward to the degree that you disagree. Note the relative position of each participant after each move. What might this tell you about your group? Here are the statements:

   a. Before people can be realistic about what their academic strengths and challenges are, they must first be able to accept all aspects of their psyche.

   b. As children, autistics typically need a parent or other adult to speak on their behalf; however, as a young adult student, it becomes essential.

   c. "What good is a diagnosis when I am really not 'disabled'? I can figure out how to go to college without a diagnosis, lots of people do."

   d. By rejecting all diagnoses outright, we end up claiming our own individual identity at the expense of downplaying the amazing intellectual diversity found in the human population as a whole.

4. What role did Veronica's friend play in her self-disclosure? Can you understand why Veronica spoke up in class during that first incident? Can you appreciate why her friend did what she did?

5. Controversy often arises between those who seek to cure autism and those who promote autistic rights. One faction may see autism chiefly as a disability whereas the other sees it as a mark of human diversity. Is there room to express both views as part of the reality of autism? How might this happen that best promotes the success of students with autism, and the colleges and universities that seek to educate them?

6. What do you think, and how do you feel, about the way Byron and his friends got to cut the line at Disneyland? If you are autistic, have you ever done something similar? If you are not, have you ever wondered if someone you worked with was doing something similar?

7. Give examples of how you have seen autism claimed as a key part of someone's identity in joyful, life-giving ways.

Intimacy

Who Will Dance With Me?

A program or an ally can provide tools to unmask the "hidden curriculum" of social rules, but in the end, the student has to step out and find friends and dates on his or her own terms and learn to cooperate with his or her instructors. If you have been to one, take yourself back to your first dance or party. Can you recall how awkward it felt? Do you remember how different genders grouped up? And how, for the most part, no one really knew what to do, let alone say, to someone?

We also refer to Erikson's sixth stage, "intimacy vs. isolation," as "genitality." According to Erikson, procreation is the driving instinct behind this stage. Although such a psychosexual term seems to throw us back to century-old theories of psychoanalysis, common sense still suggests that students in this stage are indeed concerned with how they will make friends, find dates, and cooperate with their instructors. Without a successful resolution to stage six, the danger students face is they may be drawn toward *isolation* and even exclusivity rather than *intimacy*.

Intimacy in our culture and time is still a word loaded with sexual overtones; however, successfully finding persons with whom to have sex is not the only resolution of the genitality stage—no matter what pop culture promotes. For Erikson, "intimacy" is a very broad term. Young adults achieve balance in this stage in many ways. This stage is resolved only when he or she is able to seek, find, and make friends in one's adult life. Intimacy occurs on a one-to-one basis as well as in a group. One can have intimate and detailed knowledge of a subject, place, or historical event. Intimacy is a quality associated with something that is warm and comfortable to the individual. For a college student, intimacy can take many forms, from socializing with dorm mates or college clubs to gaining expertise in a particular field of study or reading a favorite novel on a comfy chair in the library.

Intimacy is about all kinds of relationships, and significant human relationships in college include not only lovers but also friends, fellow students, and even instructors. Erikson calls such people "partners in competition and in cooperation" (1997). Potential partners may include classmates, friends, roommates, teammates, professors, and academic coaches as well as dates. In order for partnerships like these to arise, it is important to understand a little more about how students on the spectrum may struggle to read social cues and apply fixed rules to the unfamiliar, flexible situations in which they find themselves during their first year of college.

HIDDEN CURRICULUM, UNWRITTEN RULES, AND COMPLETELY NEW CONTEXTS!

Adult students on the spectrum may have problems behaving in the college setting in ways that mirror what others expect. These issues arise from both criterion A and criterion B of the diagnostic criteria for autism spectrum disorder (American Psychiatric Association, 2013). Criterion A suggests that students may have not learned how to read the social expectations and cues. Criterion B indicates that the person with autistic cognition may prefer rules without exceptions, making it difficult for them to adapt to social situations with all their ambiguity. Beyond both of these, it is important to remember that the novelty of being in higher education for the first time throws everyone off, not just those who are on the spectrum. Research and the experiences of adults on the spectrum have contributed to three ways of characterizing how students with autism may struggle as they seek to connect to others in the college setting: the hidden curriculum, the unwritten rules of social relationships, and context blindness.

Hidden Curriculum

Brenda Smith Myles and colleagues propose the first categorization, called the "hidden curriculum," (Myles, Trautman, & Schelvan, 2004). This theory suggests that neurotypical individuals learn how to read social cues during childhood without ever being explicitly taught. Since the early 2000s, the general body of research has supported the idea that neurotypical children acquire everything, from maintaining personal space to reading emotions through facial expressions, "automatically" when they are very young. This is not the case for children with autism. If a person does not acquire these abilities in childhood, then he or she may have to face the baffling consequences of not knowing how to get through social situations as an adult student.

The concept of hidden curriculum has spawned many approaches to teaching those on the spectrum. It suggests that people with autism can learn how to interpret body language, inflection, and other aspects of social communication if they learn how to make these aspects of language explicit. One critique of this approach is that people with autistic cognition often rely on rules and guidelines to process their social approach in the world, but that the rules that a neurotypical person follows to succeed gracefully in a social setting are not clear, concise, or easily understood.

Unwritten Rules

Temple Grandin and Sean Barron set out to create a set of rules to address this criticism. In their book, *Unwritten Rules of Social Relationships,* these authors—who are both adults with autism—provide a list of 10 rules that they see as governing social relationships (2005). These are worth looking at, whether you are neurotypical or autistic:

Rule #1	Rules are not absolute. They are situation- and people-based.
Rule #2	Not everything is equally important in the grand scheme of things.
Rule #3	Everyone in the world makes mistakes. It doesn't have to ruin your day.
Rule #4	Honesty is different from diplomacy.
Rule #5	Being polite is appropriate in any situation.
Rule #6	Not everyone who is nice to me is my friend.
Rule #7	People act differently in public than they do in private.

Rule #8	Know when you're turning people off.
Rule #9	"Fitting in" is often tied to looking and sounding like you fit in.
Rule #10	People are responsible for their own behaviors.

Autistic students and adults can benefit from choosing a rule, reading the exposition on it within the book, and doing some critical thinking about how the rule applies to their own lives. Because the authors parse out the rules and the exceptions from their own life experiences, this technique speaks to just how flexible a person needs to be in order to thrive in a variety of social situations. Although the rules provide powerful insights into how to read the hidden curriculum, digesting them is not enough. Students still have the desire and the challenge of how to make new friends in a new setting as socially complex as the college campus.

Successfully navigating the social complexities of college requires more than just understanding that there may be a hidden curriculum. It also requires more than just understanding a set of rules that govern that curriculum. It requires an understanding of the contexts in which social interaction occurs on campus. The social world can be slippery—it sometimes seems that exceptions govern it, more than rules.

Context Blindness

Recent theories about autism emphasize that students with autism do not use context to make meaning in the same way as neurotypical people (Vermeulen, 2012). Because social cues and rules shift according to context, and college is a completely new context for college freshman, it is that much more difficult for a student who has just arrived on a college campus to figure out how to behave. College plunges young people into social situations that they have not often experienced. For instance, rule number four—"honesty is different than diplomacy"—looks one way when giving a potential new friend a compliment while playing video games and looks another way when giving a classmate in algebra class a compliment on the first day of school.

Resolving stage six, then, is a very complex endeavor. It involves finding ways to address a social language that is sometimes hidden from those with autism and learn social expectations using rules that change according to contexts—contexts that these students may not have yet even encountered within their brand new setting.

DATING

Before "going there," it is thought-provoking to note that, although all students are seeking to create close, intimate relationships in college—according to the aforementioned Eriksonian definition of that word—the specific relationship we call "dating" does not rise to the top of every student's concerns. In fact, it is possible that dating and romance may not be high on their list of concerns at all. For example, Temple Grandin, arguably the most famous autistic person in the world today, wrote,

> Some people with autism don't understand or experience any sort of emotional attachment or romantic love. ... I was one of those people; I never had a crush on a movie star growing up. In high school, it was beyond my comprehension why other girls squealed with delight when The Beatles appeared on *The Ed Sullivan Show*. Even today, romantic love is just not part of my life. And you know what? That's okay with me. (Grandin & Barron, 2005, p. 41)

Still, for some students on the spectrum, dating remains one of the most sought-after and confusing aspects of social competency. I am always amused by the thought of me, a happily married, middle-aged man, teaching a bunch of nineteen and twenty-somethings how to successfully date; I suspect that if my students were all neurotypical, chances are I would be the last person they would come to with their dating questions. Despite these facts, several positive sources are available to turn to when the subject of how to date comes up.

Jed Baker's (2005) curriculum book, *Preparing for Life*, defines dating as: "Going out with someone in an identified setting such as a restaurant, cinema, or cultural event with the intent of getting to know them better to see if you both would be interested in developing a romantic relationship" (253). This is a thoughtful definition, but it also begs several questions. What do you do on a date? How do you act? Who pays? How do you choose where to go? The amount of hidden curriculum in any "identified public setting" can be staggering. What's more, the unwritten social rules one follows at the cinema are quite different from the ones at a rock concert or an art opening. The way you act at a table in White Castle has almost nothing in common with the way people expect you to act at a high-end French restaurant. So how does a cousin, roommate, or other ally even begin to coach a student who chooses this path to dating?

One way to begin is to try to make the rules of dating etiquette comprehensible and unambiguous. This may be challenging in a society as culturally diverse and individualistic as ours; like so much else in the social world, the rules change from setting to setting and from one generation to the next. Students who are now in college simply do not operate by the same social rules that once governed Western society. Consider Leo Tolstoy's "The Death of Ivan Ilyich," written in 1886:

> Miss Praskovya Fyodorovna was of good noble stock and not bad looking; there was a bit of money. Ivan Ilyich had his salary; she, he hoped, would have as much. A good family; she was a sweet, pretty, and perfectly respectable woman. To say that Ivan Ilyich married because he loved his bride and found her sympathetic to his view of life would be as incorrect as to say that he married because people of his society approved of this match. Ivan Ilyich married out of both considerations: he did something pleasant for himself acquiring such a wife, and at the same time, he did what highly placed people considered right.
>
> And so Ivan Ilyich got married. (1886/2009, 51)

This Victorian approach had many drawbacks—especially for women—but the rules were clear and certain. Today's approach to dating is far less consistent, based more on individual choice than on social norm. People once found their life partner from the immediate community in which they grew up—family, church, or friends. Today most men and women work, and many more go to college than ever before. As a result, mates are now found most often in the setting one chooses as a young adult—whether an office or a classroom. Companies often have expectations or policies about dating in the workplace, but colleges usually do not (beyond a general ban on students and instructors fraternizing). Thus almost no academic communities, except perhaps very conservative ones, have explicit rules to help those who would prefer some guidelines about dating, in spite of the fact that students are in the midst of resolving stage six, laying claim to the responsibility for what it means to love and be loved.

I know of only one student-led experiment in the 1980s at Antioch College that may be an exception to this. The "Antioch dating rule" was cited into the 1990s, and has come up again in contemporary discussions about college dating and consent ('Ask First at Antioch,' 1993). Among other things, the rule required all students to ask permission at all stages of the dating process—from "Where would you like to go?" to "May I kiss you?" and beyond. It seems sort of anachronistic thirty years later, but rules like this, if accepted by the entire postsecondary community in a non-legalistic way, might go a long way to assisting students with autism as they trek through the whole dating experience.

The 1980s are long gone, and the Antioch College statement is an article of the past. Currently, we leave the rules of dating up to the individuals involved, and the assumption seems to be that all students will pick up how to interact just by being around others who are interacting. This assumption seldom works for people with autistic cognition. In recent news, people have put a great deal of emphasis on curbing campus sexual assault through, among other things, expanding the conversation on what consensual sex is (or is not). This is an extremely important movement for all young adult students to take part in. It is strongly encouraged that this conversation begin with all students (neurotypical and ASD) at home and in their high schools well before they come to campus and join the conversation there as well.

Without clear guidelines for those who would like to have them, dating can become too much to handle. In response to the anxiety (and sometimes, even shutdown) this confusion can cause, some autistic adults are beginning to explore and discuss a preference for online dating. Several sites are establishing discussions and protocols for people on the spectrum concerning dating (e.g., Spectrum Singles, https://www.spectrumsingles.com/). Whether autistic people wish to date only other autistic people through such sites is an open question, but it is clear that many coaches and parents may not be equipped to direct their autistic friends and family members through the world of online dating.

Friendship First

The rules and the context of dating in college can be perplexing to students with autism; however, the issue may be approached in another way—seek friendship first. Dating in our culture sometimes springs from the soil of friendship, and although friendship can be an elusive concept for many autistics to grasp at first, friendship concerns are even stronger than dating concerns among the cohorts I have taught. Many of these students report difficulty in knowing how to start or maintain conversations, when to listen and when to talk, and sometimes even how to physically stand in the presence of those with whom they would like to become friends, let alone date. Instead of beginning with a list of social dating rules, the friendship-first approach pairs a student's friendship concerns with concrete, visual activities that might lead to closer personal connections. This may take some convincing.

The first thing to clearly state is that a link exists between friendship and romance. This is not always easy to grasp because so much of popular culture depicts romance as chiefly sexual and coming out of nowhere—across a crowded room. As a result, students have a variety of reactions to the idea of romance. They run the gamut from dreamy to strictly biological. I have had students who told me something like, "It will happen, and when it does I will know it." I have also had students who declared, "It's just for the purpose of procreation, messy and animalistic." These attitudes and others like them make it harder to help students on the spectrum see the connection between having friends and finding someone with whom they wish to spend their lives.

Once the link is established between friendships and dating, the next step is to begin with an examination of relationship types. An elementary school–age curriculum called *Circles* (Stanfield, n.d.) can be adapted for this purpose. (The Circles program is described in some detail in the Appendix. For a full overview of this curriculum, visit http://autismteacher.blog.com/2011/03/24/circles-social-program.) In this exercise, students are asked to draw, or if they are more kinesthetic, to create a huge set of concentric circles on the floor. They then place themselves in the center. The moderator then asks them to put others in concentric circles out from where they stand and to label each arc. Students can choose their own labels, but these are suggestions: Best Friend, Close Friend, Friend, Classmate, Acquaintance, and Stranger.

The more control the student has over the labels used and the people placed, the better the exercise will turn out for them. For instance, family members are included in the first circle only some of the time, but not always. Usually the student places a name or two in the next closest circles, and sometimes titles or names like "my Algebra teacher" go in the outer circle. Classmates, and others whose names the student does not know, usually fall into the outermost ring. Conversation about why different people are placed in different circles takes place, and then students are asked if they might wish to move any person into a closer circle—perhaps a close friend they would like to date—or push anyone out into a farther one.

The third step is to demonstrate that we build our friendships upon shared experiences, experiences that ultimately lead to shared meaning. This introduction to the exercise, or one like it, demonstrates the concept of how brains are "wired."

> When I share the experience of shaking hands with someone after class, a set of connections to that person is built inside my brain. If we then go to the coffee shop, where the aroma of fresh roasted coffee and freshly baked pastries intermingles with a conversation about how much we both love the video game *Call of Duty*, a whole new set of connections is created in my brain (and in the brain of my new friend). For me, this cluster of connections may also link up with how the room back home where I keep my game console looks, and then with what it was like to get that console on my birthday last month, and so on, and so on.

Eventually something both mystical and mechanical has happened—a great many brain connections have been formed in the brains of both people, and when enough are built up, the two become friends.

Of course, finding the person who shares a mutual interest in blintzes and role-playing games may require some preparation and even risk taking. Where do you go to meet people on campus who like pastry? Are you willing to take the chance to shake that person's hand to begin with, let alone meet them at the Student Union? A social skills curriculum based on how to start a conversation, maintain a conversation, not get off track, and end the conversation may still be useful—however, the goal of the coursework is not to memorize a bunch of opening lines, but to establish a common ground from which intimacy and friendship can grow and become understood.

Once students can elaborate on their circles with finesse and confidence, they can begin to imagine what people on the circles they want to move closer to them, and whom they might now see as farther out. They may even decide to try to start dating one of their friends.

I'm Dating My Best Friend

> I went out with Jesse last weekend! I cannot believe how much fun we had. I'm already really starting to think about what our kids will look like.

Such discussions can come quickly to a person who is "in love" for the first time. For many autistic students who have had little or no dating experience before, it is always a temptation to slam the door shut on the intimacy vs. isolation stage, call it resolved, and never go out there again. New love is both pretty to look at and joyful to feel; however, working on strengthening a relationship is an essential part of every adult's quest for true intimacy. This is true for neurotypical adults as well as those on the spectrum. For people with autism, timing issues and "mind-blindness" are two challenges they may experience as they seek to strengthen their close relationships.

Jed Baker's (2005) guidebook provides some very practical tips on how to be cautious about not going too fast and taking the time to read the signals. He builds his case on having strong communication skills and demonstrates that what deepens a relationship is time and deliberation. Because people with autism often have concerns and even anxiety about time, it is important to discuss the idea that deepening friendships through listening takes time.

Good communication begins by taking the time to listen to the other person. One exercise to demonstrate good listening skills is to construct a toy "telephone" from two paper cups and a string. If the group is not inclined to be so creative, a drawing of this contraption is usually enough to ring the bell of memory, and students will often recall having made such a toy before. The key to such a communication device is this: you can listen, or you can talk, but you cannot do both.

It may be necessary for a person to assign a number of times or minutes arbitrarily to the process, but the idea that time needs to be part of the equation is essential. A person is either listening or talking; trust between companions, leading toward deeper friendship, will happen only when each person has the opportunity to send a complete message when it is their turn and to feel it is completely received by the other (Ellis, 2012, p. 147).

In order to deepen a relationship, it may be necessary to address what Baron-Cohen (1997) has called "mind-blindness"—that is, the lack of ability to see a situation or an idea from another's point of view. Mind-blindness is not just a trait of the autistic person's brain wiring. In fact, mind-blindness is often at the center of human disputes as naïve as a seventh-grade "break-up" or as dire as a civil war. Autistic people do not have a monopoly on mind-blindness, but wherever it is in play, communication becomes problematic.

Deepening our friendship with another person—moving them closer to the center of our circle—requires that we first understand that their need for love, acceptance, and respect may vary from our own. Furthermore, the language they use to express their need and the words they hope we will say to help them fulfill their need may be very different from our language as well. There are plenty of books and popular techniques printed on this; I find that Chapman's (1992) concept of "love languages" is helpful here because it focuses on emotional love and how the need for it varies from one person to another. There is no way to "frontload" these kinds of lessons. As allies, coaches, and autistics who have learned that ourselves, we can only promise to be available as our loved ones and students on the spectrum set out to make their own relationships and ways in the world.

Understanding and accepting a friend or lover's point of view is a deeply personal skill set that leads to intimacy and varies from relationship to relationship. However, learning to understand and accept a professor's point of view is also an element of stage six resolution. Many of the partners we have in life will not become our best friends, yet we still need to learn to cooperate with them and maybe even compete fairly and respectfully against them. Professors and instructors make up one category of these kinds of partners. The following section begins with an exercise designed to provide guidance for students so that they may understand their instructor's point of view.

COOPERATION AND COMPETITION: STUDENT–INSTRUCTOR INTERACTION

"From My Point of View" Exercise

Invite two or three instructors to participate; introductions are made among them and the students. The room is set up with two chairs set back to back. The participants gather around this stage or "fishbowl" so that they can see the action. Two volunteers, one instructor and one student, each take their place in the chairs. One person gets a simple preprinted picture. The other person sits with a pencil and paper. Using only direction words (up, down, and so on) the one with the simple picture tells the other how to draw what they are seeing. When the drawing is complete, the two compare their work. Each participant answers questions such as the following:

- How close (or far apart) were the original image and the drawing?
- On a scale of 1–10, how frustrating was it to draw (or describe) the image?
- The rules were to only use direction words. What other words might have eased this?
- How was the describer's point of view different from the drawer's?

The second part of the exercise expands the general lesson by substituting classroom language for the simple preprinted picture. Student–Instructor pairs take turns reading and discussing an assignment or simple concept from a lecture. This is a good time to introduce the importance of using exact language and encouraging the student to ask additional questions if he or she suspects the professor is coming from another point of view. For instance:

- The instructor says, "Everyone got that?" From the instructor's point of view, this means *do you have any questions about the whole lesson?*
- From the student's point of view, he was just asked if he wrote down the last word the instructor put on the board.
- The student thinks "Yes," and the instructor never knows that the student did not understand anything that came previously in the lecture.

A more effective way to do this would have been for the instructor to say, "There is a review quiz next week on today's lecture material, so I will now take questions about anything that was covered today in class. Please raise your hands and ask away..." (Boucher & Oehler, 2013).

For the next part, the students and professors divide into pairs and repeat the activity. It is a really great idea to switch roles as well. Have some of the students take the instructor's role, and the instructors sit in as students. Insight flourishes when people act.

Finally, remember to use the "fishbowl," which is made up of all the other participants in the room listening in or watching the exercise. It is an essential component for several reasons. First, it allows for "shy" participants to become actively involved. Not everyone likes to be on the stage. Second, the fishbowl helps set up more rounds of the activity by encouraging observers to shape the content of the next role-play (e.g., what if we looked at a syllabus? I never understand them) In this way, observations and ideas coming from the fishbowl broaden the points of view being brought to the exercise—and that is what the entire activity is trying to do.

There is one caution. When doing point-of-view exercises, it is important to reinforce the wholeness and positive sides of being yourself, on or off the spectrum. No one point of view is always correct or on target. Communication issues will always be part of every relationship. The main point of "From My Point of View" is to make room for people to tell their side of the story and for others to make room for listening to what each person has to say. (If role-playing is not your thing, try *Rory's Story Cubes*. They are pictographic dice used to tell stories and share points of view in a safe, game-like manner.)

Adult–Adult Relationships

One thing a new college student discovers early on is that their instructor is not exactly their friend. Successful students learn quickly that student–instructor relationships are different from relationships whose point is to "make friends." Another thing new college students discover early on is that the relationships they have with their professors are not like the ones they had with their high school or grade school teachers, either. The difference is that they are now adults, not children. Diagramming different kinds of adult-to-adult relationships may be one useful way for a student to begin to understand the power differential involved in these relationships.

K–12 Classroom	Campus Life (Peers)	College Classroom
ADULT ➡ child	ADULT ⬅➡ ADULT	ADULT ⬅➡ ADULT
TEACHER ➡ pupil	CLASSMATE ⬅➡ CLASSMATE	PROFESSOR ⬅➡ college student

The POWER resides in the person indicated on the chart in all capital letters, but the arrows additionally indicate that negotiations can sometimes go both ways. In K–12 classrooms, all the power rests in the teacher's hands because this is an adult-child relationship. Furthermore, the pupil or child has no recourse for negotiating a change in the relationship's power dynamic. This is not the case once the "pupil" turns into an adult student.

First of all, as an adult participating with peers in various campus-life activities, the power in all of campus-life relationships is equally distributed—each partner can stay or go as he or she pleases, and each partner can attempt to negotiate a change in the dynamic or reject a change being offered by the other. (If you are a student experiencing a campus-life social situation where you do not feel this to be the case, go to someone for support immediately). Furthermore, as an adult participating in the college classroom, the power is also open to negotiation. The instructor has the power to set the parameters for the grade and to run the class as he or she sees fit; however, the student has the power to ask the teacher to change his or her approach to make it more comprehensible or to drop the course or the section if that does not happen. Although the college hires the professor to run the class, the student is paying for the class and ultimately can choose to make a change provided he or she is willing and able to handle the consequences of that change.

As with the hidden curriculum discussed earlier in the chapter, this is sometimes new information for a student on the spectrum. Dealing with it requires understanding a few unwritten rules and adopting a strategy for interacting with an instructor in the context of an adult-to-adult working relationship.

Four Rules for Students to Consider When They Interact with Their Instructors

Rule #1

Despite the power differential and potentially unknown social curriculum involved in student–instructor interaction, *I strongly advise students to get in front of their professors and build a relationship with them.* (The Appendix includes a Student–Instructor Interaction Checklist that students may use when writing a script or to obtain instructor feedback after their first meeting. There are also some additional sample scripts to help students prepare for that meeting.)

At large research universities with literally hundreds of students in a lecture hall, this may be nearly impossible. In such cases, autistic students should make relationships with the teacher assistants, tutors, and/or fellow students assigned to the same study group.

Students with autism may become anxious if they believe the only academic relationships available are based primarily on social situations like meeting instructors. A college usually provides teachers, tutors, and study groups—sometimes belonging to such a group is even required of first-year students. The challenge for a student on the spectrum is that all of these are built on social connections. This may feel like a "double whammy" for many students on the spectrum: first, you tell me I have to take certain courses, and then you tell me that my best way to get through them is to create a relationship with a tutor or join another social group? Some students may be open to this idea, but some may shut down even anticipating the demands of it, if not actually when the time comes to get support in-person.

At smaller colleges or in smaller classes, they should learn the instructor's office location and hours, email address, and office phone number on the first day. This information is usually on the class syllabus. They should speak with the instructor by one of these means during the first 2 weeks of the semester. They should expect to be a little anxious. If this is the case, asking an ally or academic coach to assist in the process may help. They can go as far as accompanying the student to the meeting or being there when they dial the phone. The ally can also help the student write out a list of things to share (often called a script) when conversing with the instructor. If it helps, remember that the best instructors welcome contact of this sort with their students—it helps them be better teachers. The student should go to the meeting with questions to ask and be prepared to carefully share relevant information with the professor about how autism affects them.

Sample Student Script Developed with an Academic Coach

I have Asperger's syndrome. It is my goal to get a high "B" in my classes, but it does affect me.

This sometimes affects my ability to concentrate, and I do not always show that I am concentrating even when I am. In order to let you know that I am paying attention, I will write with one pencil and have another pencil on the desk with me. If I do not have that other pencil out, it means I am having trouble concentrating that day. In order to hold myself accountable for those times, I will get notes from a classmate and listen to my recording of the lecture later when my mind focuses.

Sometimes small things that most neurotypical people would not even notice distract me. If this happens, I will try to ignore it. If it is a noise, I will wear my earplugs (I always have them with me). I can still hear the teacher when I have them in. They just block out the small annoying sounds.

Today I am asking you to allow me to do this. I would like to get feedback from you in three weeks again to see how this plan is working.

Rule #2

No matter what sort of support you seek, accessing it usually requires at least some interaction with people you may or may not know. In addition to support from a coach, the student can also find online supports that can help them navigate the class. You can do this as soon as the student is able to receive the class syllabus; often, professors include such online material in their syllabus and may even require using it. In addition to drop-in writing centers, some colleges have online writing centers that a student on the spectrum may be more comfortable using. Remember that humans still run non-human support. Often, you can access online material through advocates in the college disability services department, for instance, and helpful people wearing headsets staff online writing centers. My own college and many others provide speech-to-text support free of charge to qualifying students.

Rule #3

Some of the unwritten rules of student–instructor interaction are actually written down. You will find them in your institution's student handbook. They include rules about behavior, grades, registration, and dropping classes. They may be woven into policies about Internet use on campus computers or grievance procedures connected to the student code of conduct. Before coming to campus as a student, read the student handbook and other publications about disability services, records and registration, student support services, and any others your campus puts out. Schools also sometimes send related information via periodic emails. If you have any questions or wonder what to pay special attention to, go to a staff person or an older student that you know for answers.

Rule #4

College is not just the time to become academically and vocationally ready; it is the time to become socially adept, as well. Autism can never be the reason for a young adult not to take responsibility for finding others to work with and even love. We task higher education not just with academic preparation, but also assisting students as they practice being adults. Becoming an adult includes developing skill sets that lead a person to working relationships that are close, familiar, and affectionate. Our entire lives, we have opportunities to seek, find, and make colleagues and friends. How this happens is part of the mystery and wonder of life, no matter what our intellectual differences may be.

FOUR PRINCIPLES FOR COACHING STUDENTS TO RESOLVE STAGE SIX

There are four principles to follow in resolving stage six (affiliational love) for people on the autism spectrum.

Create concrete connections. Whether you are using concentric circles, brain diagrams, games, charts, or even marbles to illustrate your point, remember that relationships include language processing but go way beyond words.

Practice reciprocity when teaching relationship-building on a campus. Do not just focus on students with autism. Be sure that neurotypical students, advisors, and professors are included in the practice. If communication coaching teaches us nothing else, remember that it takes both people to create a misunderstanding—the blame never falls on one person alone.

Insist on formal feedback and real-life relevance. The resolution of stage six happens out in the world as young people go about the new environment of higher education learning to find others to fill in their social circle. It is easy for them get "lost on campus" and not find ways or means to practice what they have learned. To avoid this, coaches and students can agree to gather data that hold one another accountable for being honest and moving forward. Feedback can be formal without being oppressive. It can happen in student-led clubs (Chapter 10) or group settings. (Many psychology practices and centers for autism support springing up around the country use this "group" technique to get at the hidden curriculum and make it explicit.) Feedback can also happen one-on-one. A brief form is the only thing needed to help students discover where they begin and how they are doing as they attend campus activities and official appointments. Here are examples:

FIG. 5.1 Example Activity Checklist with Comments

My Name: Joe S. Student	
Activity, Group, or Event: Brenda Lee's Restaurant (Run by Culinary Dept.)	
Date or Time: Wednesday, February 4, 2015	
Comments: what did I do; who did I meet; what did I like; what do I wonder about; what will I do next as a result of this. (Use additional paper if necessary)	
What did I do?	I went to the student-run restaurant in the basement of the Student Center Hall for lunch.
Who did I meet? (Name)	I met Joy and Doreen from financial aid.
What did I like? (or dislike)	The food was fantastic! I had salmon pappiotte (salmon steamed in paper) and yummy fried bread. It only cost $4.00!
What do I wonder about?	I wonder how they can make such great food for so little money. I also wonder what will be on the menu next Thursday.
What will I do next as a result?	I plan on going back next week.
Other comments	They only do this for about six Thursdays each quarter, so get there while you can. Oh yeah, and Dylan was there too.

FIG. 5.2   Example Advisor Appointment Feedback Form

My Name: _____
Person Meeting With: _____
Date and Time: _____

Short Summary—What I asked; What I learned; What I do next
Asked:
Would you please tell me about the Associate of Art track vs. the Associate of Science Track?
Could you help me develop a quarter-by-quarter plan based on our discussion?
Learned:
The Associate of Art or of Science Tracks are both designed to align with transfer options to a 4-year school. They require many general courses but have lots of electives later on.
What I do next:
1. Change my major to Associate of Art through the registration window.
2. Go to the Transfer Fair to get information on at least three possible 4-year schools next week.
*Blank versions of these forms are available in the Appendix.

Model intimate relationships, with the autistic differences pointed out.

For instance, modeling the idea that "good communication takes time," without considering that the concept of time may be a problem for an autistic person, would not work. Additionally, the things we call "autistic challenges," such as the theory of mind and the theory of context blindness, are actually all part of humanity. Autistics may be the ones who know these challenges best, but this does not doom them to a solitary life. It is precisely because they feel these challenges more acutely that people on the autism spectrum can become the best friends, boyfriends, girlfriends, husbands, wives, or diplomats that anyone ever had.

THIS ROMEO AND JULIET HAVE ASPERGER'S SYNDROME

Systematic communication between autistic college students and their allies, coaches, and friends can lead to success in college. The sooner in their journey to school, the more often allies and students check in with each other, the more successful in college they can be.

Yet it is important to remember that no amount of therapeutic wisdom will ever allow one person to control how, with whom or even whether another person forms relationships. Only the students themselves will be able ultimately to handle the consequences of what they choose. Teachers, allies, and even loving parents help their loved ones best when they encourage and empower, and do not try to control or pontificate. Furthermore, the label "autism" is not the only source of explaining or describing where a person's decisions have come from. Consider this example:

 JULIET

She had ridden the roller coaster of the first quarter of college. She was photogenic, articulate in public, and had held a part-time job for almost a year. The team decided that if there was going to be a "poster girl" for the program, it would be this student. We were all very fond of her.

Then, partway into what was already becoming another academically successful quarter for her, she called to tell us that she would not be back to college. She was moving in with her boyfriend, a coworker from the office where she worked. That was it. Her family disapproved, the team was in shock, but the student was resolved.

For a while, we threw around various theories that we tried to connect to the way Asperger's syndrome affected our star student. It was her need for sameness, ran one theory. There had been too much change too fast, and this fellow was a way for her to get back into a routine and setting that was the same for her. This theory did not hold water at all, however; she had been involved in college for months by this point. We knew better, yet we continued to

> explain away what we saw by blaming it on her Asperger's syndrome.
>
> Then one day a woman on team said, "She fell in love. And when you are nineteen and you fall in love, you move in with your boyfriend."

Asperger's syndrome did not make this star student as clear a communicator as either she or the team fancied she was, but it was not the cause of her decision to leave school and start a deep relationship. Many extraordinary pressures and concerns contributed to the decisions she made, yet we could not help asking ourselves how we might have coached her better so that she could resolve her stage six issues and still manage to remain a successful college student.

 QUESTIONS

1. How are friendship and dating related? How do these two concepts change with a person's age?

2. What rules about dating have you heard? What rules about dating have you heard at your college? As these are shared, what differences in these rules emerge based upon the gender, age, ethnicity, or background of the members of the group sharing them?

3. Would dating be easier if we all shared the same rules? Why do you agree or disagree with the Antioch College rules?

4. How might "Juliet" have been coached to stay in school? Would earlier communication between her and her academic coaches have led to a different outcome?

5. Under what conditions, if ever, is it an academic coach's business what a student does with his or her love life?

Accommodations

TOO MUCH SOUND IN THE SOUND LAB (NOTES FROM A MEDIATION)

Present: Advocate, professor, student, and mom

Purpose: All parties express an interest in "resolving" an incident that occurred in the sound engineering lab the week prior to this meeting.

Description: Student began by describing a recent incident where he was overwhelmed by too much sound stimulation, so he told the professor that he was going to "hit someone" and then he took himself to another corner of the room to "relax and meditate and get back under control."

Action: Professor was concerned by what student said (in the code of conduct, saying that you are going to hit someone clearly indicates a need to take action). The presenting student went to an area where another student was working. Professor was concerned this student might be in danger of being hit, so she asked student politely to go out in the hall by himself. The professor then explained her request to the presenting student, and the student told the professor he understood and complied. Then the professor called Disability Services, who referred her to Public Safety. At that point, the professor called Public Safety. Presenting student was "shocked" by this and deemed it "unfair and possibly discriminatory," because the professor knows "I have the intellectual disability of autism."

Aspects: Professor, student, and advocate discussed several aspects of the incident from both sides and finally asked the student's mother to enter the conversation. Her summation was, "The words he chose to say were at the heart of the problem, not what he actually did."

THE DREAM OF AUTISM-SPECIFIC ACCOMMODATIONS

Incidents like this one describe how ASD symptoms impair a student with autism's ability to succeed in college. Most disability services departments offer supports like reduced distraction testing and extra time on exams; digital versions of textbooks and class materials; alternative note-taking or digitally recorded lectures; sometimes scribe or read-aloud services; and of course braille and American sign language interpreters for students with visual or hearing impairments. Although some of these may be helpful for a student with autism, none of them are directly designed for students on the spectrum. So the question becomes—what supports can we offer that explicitly address the effects of ASD?

In order to begin to answer this question, it is necessary to note the difference between what a student in K–12 legally receives and how that changes drastically once the child becomes eighteen years old, when we consider them an adult learner. This is not a treatise on disability law, but, briefly put, K–12 public schools in the United States have a legal mandate to ensure that a student with a disability receives two things: individually designed interventions, and the least-restrictive environment available.

The journey for many students with autism begins when a student is still in the K–12 system. Usually a teacher or parent requests an intervention team observation because they believe their student is not performing as well as he or she should on ordinary tasks, or is not meeting expected grade level requirements.

If the team suspects a disability, then the next step is often an evaluation—sometimes known as a multi-factored evaluation or, alternatively, an evaluation team report. This evaluation includes both professionals within the school system—such as a school psychologist, speech pathologist, occupational therapist, or physical therapist—and sometimes professionals outside the school system, such as a medical doctor, therapist, or psychiatrist. The results of this evaluation travel to another team that consists of the parents or guardians, student, intervention teachers, regular education teachers, and the district representative tasked with approving and paying for "special services" within that system. This group writes a goal-driven legal document on behalf of the student addressing his or her identified needs, which we call the *Individualized Education Program*, or IEP.

A great many hours of workshops, lectures, and careers have been devoted to IEP design and implementation in the past three or four decades. Many refinements have come along, but the gist remains the same. The IEP is the legal contract that holds public school systems accountable for how (and why) their K–12 program supports a student with a disability. The IEP design contains reasonable, obtainable, observable, and measurable goals that can be changed or modified at the behest of the IEP team and as the child matures through grade school and high school. Because they are subject to laws written for minors, IEPs may contain both "accommodations" and/or "modifications."

Accommodations in K–12 include supports such as ensuring the student with a visual impairment always has a seat in the front row or allowing an autistic student to take "sensory breaks" outside of the classroom on a regular basis to prevent meltdowns. Accommodations are usually simple and do not alter the curriculum. Modifications, on the other hand, do alter the curriculum and often the expectations associated with it. An example of a modification might be requiring answers to only eight out of ten questions on a quiz from the student with the disability. Accommodations and modifications together give support to K–12 students; however, by law, adult learners do not receive modifications.

In the past decade or two, the emphasis has switched from how we do interventions on a day-to-day basis in a particular school building, to what kinds of outcomes will result because of the intervention in the students' lives. We call this "transition," and it is now a key element in the IEP process of most states. Transition planning may begin as early as the student's first IEP. It must begin by 16. Regardless of when it begins, transition planning may continue through the age of 22 if deemed necessary by the IEP team.

We used to write IEPs with little influence from the legislature. Now, they are based more and more on legalized standards written and adapted by the states (so-called "State Standards," or more recently, "Common Core"), and are measured, more or less, by test scores and graduation rates. Furthermore, many state school systems and individual teachers are now "graded" based on the data from tests and samples of what graduates are doing one year after their high school graduation. Are they employed? Are they attending postsecondary school or a training program? Are they doing neither? This is why the results of National Longitudinal Transition Study-2, mentioned earlier, and information like it is so influential.

The important point to make here is that it is incumbent upon the public school districts and their teachers and personnel to ensure that K–12 students obtain a public education. The legal precedent for an adult learner is different. Education providers for adult learners are only required to "level the playing field" and allow equal access for their students with disabilities. In the midst of this dilemma, two related principle questions need to be borne in mind: How much can be generalized for the sake of academic rigor, and how much can be specified without the student receiving unfair advantage?

It is crass to say so, but in K–12, it is the teachers' job to educate students; in college, it is the student's job to get an education. Transitioning students and their families are wise to keep this in mind. Practically speaking, it means that supports like full-time aides, modified curriculum that actually changes the expectations of the course, and legally mandated IEP intervention teams are not required or financially supported for the college student, not even in the first year. If students have counted on these kinds of supports to get through high school, they will need to find new ways of obtaining the same backing and encouragement on their own when they arrive at XYZ University.

Locating support in a new setting after high school has not proven easy for students and their allies. In order to understand why it has been so difficult for students with autism to find support in postsecondary situations, we need to break down the diagnosis of autism.

DIAGNOSIS

According to the DSM-5, the "essential features of autism spectrum disorder are persistent impairment in reciprocal social communications and social interaction (criterion A)" and "restricted, repetitive patterns of behavior, interests, or activities (criterion B)" (American Psychiatric Association, 2013). The other two criteria, C and D, are categorical and discussed later in the chapter.

Summary of Diagnosis

Autism (which includes Asperger's syndrome) is a "syndrome," or collection of symptoms, with four criteria:

1. *Social/Communication*—Difficulty understanding nonverbal language, conversation, and social context. These difficulties can sometimes lead to challenges in making and keeping friends.

2. *Flexibility*—Reliance on routines, strong interests, bottom-up processing, one-to-one instead of one-to-many connections. These traits can sometimes lead to frustration and resistance to change.

3. *Early age of onset*—Symptoms present in early childhood.

4. *Functional limitations*—Symptoms together limit and impair everyday functioning.

   Autism may also include:
   - Sensory challenges like hyper- or hyporeactivity to sound, light, texture, etc.
   - Related mental health challenges such as ADHD, anxiety, and depression.

The guiding question that emerges at the intersection of criteria A and B and the legal mandates for education is this: "Do the diagnostically described 'essential features' of ASD interfere with a person's right to equal access to education?" Alternatively, in terms of the law, do the effects of ASD on this person "impair or substantially limit one or more of his or her major life activities"? (Americans with Disabilities Act Amendments Act, 2008).

There is legal precedent for education being a "major life activity," so anything that interferes with equal access to that activity is protected by decades of disability law. Furthermore, a direct parallel exists between the language of criterion D in the DSM-5 for ASD and the legal language of "impairment and limitation" (American Psychiatric Association, 2013). The DSM-5 breaks down the severity level for ASD into three levels. Level 1 (requiring support) is the least severe. Level 2 (requiring substantial support) and level 3 (requiring very substantial support) round out the current symptomology for diagnosticians. As the diagnostic criteria note, ASD is not a degenerative disorder, and severity may vary by context or change over the life of the person affected; therefore, it becomes imperative that students with ASD get a handle on how ASD affects them in the specific academic setting where they begin their college education.

Ideally, students are first able to move beyond a possibly inflexible view of themselves—in other words, they thoroughly come to understand and accept their diagnosis. They then learn new techniques to help them communicate that information with the support staff at their institution of higher education so that the staff can respond to the challenge areas effectively. Of course, this is next to impossible, because without support, a person cannot simultaneously be cognitively flexible and communicative and have deficits in both those areas as indicated by the diagnosis of autism.

The DSM-5 summary of the functional consequences of ASD states: "Extreme difficulties in planning, organization, and coping with change negatively impact academic achievement, even for students with above-average intelligence. During adulthood, these individuals may have difficulties establishing independence because of continued rigidity and difficulty with novelty" (2013, p. 57). In order to achieve these priorities, a student has to receive support. The prognosis for students without support is not positive, to say the least; yet there is no reason why students with ASD have to succumb to a failing picture of their academic future. The key is for adult students to understand what "legal accommodations" they are entitled to and to pursue those supports in ways that help them succeed.

WHERE DID "ACCOMMODATIONS" COME FROM?

One way to create beneficial change for adult students who have autism is to legislate equal access to education. Indeed, the current field of special education is rooted in the legislation known as the Americans with Disabilities Act (ADA, 1990). Most disability rights histories trace their origin to the passage of Section 504 of the 1973 Rehabilitation Act. These regulations, issued in 1977, form the basis of the ADA. At that time, the spirit of the law was providing equal access to all buildings and institutions receiving federal funds. As such, architectural accommodations—including the building of ramps on public buildings—were the first visible changes brought on by ADA guidelines. The spirit of equal access and eliminating discrimination that the ADA ensconced has advanced much further. Aspects of the 1992 revision of ADA covered disability and employment (Title I), disability and state and local government (Title II), and disability and public accommodations (Title III). As Arlene Mayerson wrote in her 1992 history of the movement, "If the ADA means anything, it means that people with disabilities will no longer be out of sight and out of mind. ... Accommodating a person with a disability is no longer a matter of charity but instead a basic issue of civil rights."

There was a time when even progressive middle and high schools reserved a room, usually somewhere near the boiler in the basement, for the "special ed class," but the momentum behind the ADA laws would eventually bring the "special kids" up to the first floor. The force behind the laws would eventually feed the educational reforms that came out at the turn of the twenty-first century, including the so-called No Child Left Behind Act of 2001 and the subsequent revisions of it. The social and allied political aspects of the disabilities movement influence educational practices and curriculum to this day. Public schools now train with equal access in mind. K–12 personnel use a curriculum that sprang from the philosophical revolution first started with the passage of Section 504, based on what we now call "universal design." Universal design, briefly put, is the philosophy that all students, not just those with labeled disabilities, benefit from curricula designed with multilayered supports built into it.

To honor the new ethic of accessibility in public education, curriculum designers began to base it more and more on a concept known as "scaffolding." In short, *scaffolding* is an educational model that structures lessons so students may accomplish something that they may not have been able to understand without said structures in place. If learning a lesson were like painting an area high on a wall, the student who is too "short" to reach that place would receive support, accommodations, and assistance (scaffolding) in order to be able to reach that high. An American cognitive psychologist named Jerome Bruner first introduced scaffolding in the 1950s. The theories of Lev Vygotsky (1978) that came along later suggest that students do most learning in what he called the zone of proximal development. This zone lies just beyond what the learner already knows, but not so far away from the learner's base of knowledge as to be too cognitively frustrating.

In this process, a novice first learns from a mentor when the mentor builds a lesson based on the active knowledge of the learner. If the expert introduces a concept too far out of the learner's zone, the learner will drop out of the lesson and never grasp it; however, if the expert presents a lesson that is too simple, the learner will become bored quickly and not stay focused on the lesson. Companies created all sorts of handy educational tools to take advantage of this new educational understanding—some are simple charts and others are as complex and elaborate as the approach to a curriculum known as "Understanding by Design (UBD). Although Vygotsky's theories were first used to explain learning and teaching among students whose cognitive ability was measured in the center of the bell curve, they eventually were taken up by professionals who worked with students at either end of the curve as well. Intervention specialists are now trained to begin with the zone of proximal development of their students, whether those students have special needs or are gifted. Scaffolding is then used to lead them on to either the next set of academic concepts, or the next zone of development.

Legislating for equal access has come a long way since the 1970s. The definition of disability, particularly as it relates to intellectual diversity, continues to develop and change. The definition of *disability* in the ADA was a physical or mental impairment that substantially limits one or more major life activities (e.g., eating, sleeping, working, mobility, or learning). However, as with all legal evolution, from the book of Leviticus to the Lombard Laws to the U.S. Constitution, subsequent arguments about the words "substantially," "limits," and especially "major life activity" continue to shape the law.

Changes to the diagnosis of autism have also occurred. Most recently, the DSM-5 collapsed several formal diagnoses, including Asperger's syndrome, into one key descriptor under the numeric heading 299.00, or "autism spectrum disorder." DSM-5 seems to account for Lorna Wing's original term autism "spectrum" by rolling the idea of severity into the newest diagnostic marker for ASD (2013).

It is essential to note that the American Psychiatric Association bases diagnosis for ASD, like most others, on the concept of functionality, and the severity of a person's limitations in "everyday functions." When it made changes in the DSM-5 that combined Asperger's syndrome and other spectrum diagnoses under the single heading of ASD, many individuals raised dissenting and cautionary voices. Not all agree that defining autism by level of severity and limitation in everyday functioning is the only or best way to proceed. Some writers took very strong stances (Murray, 2010) while others took a milder, more cautionary approach. For instance, in an open communiqué entitled "Joint ASAN-Autism Society Statement on DSM-5," two autistic self-advocacy networks commented that, "The autism spectrum is broad and diverse, including individuals with a wide range of functional needs, strengths and challenges. The DSM-5's criteria for the new, unified autism spectrum disorder diagnosis must be able to reflect that diversity and range of experience," (Received from aneeman@autisticadvocacy.org, January 31, 2012). Nearly all agreed that a few priorities be kept in mind, namely, ensuring that those who were diagnosed under DSM-IV (American Psychiatric Association, 1994) keep their diagnosis and services and that the diagnosis continue to be enhanced to include females and people of color who are underrepresented in the percentage of overall autistics.

At this point, we have yet to see how the changes in the legal definition of "disability" and in the diagnosis of autism will affect people who are actually "on the ground": diagnosticians, students, parents, and educators. The five factors that are involved in mandating services for those with autism are its undeniable prevalence among those now coming into higher education; the legal definition that will drive how institutions support those incoming students now and in the future; and the many scientific, political, and practical considerations that exist around the diagnosis of autism. Yet even as these strands sort themselves out now and in the coming years, challenges also remain about where the line falls between mandating support and enforcing the provision of support. As the old saying goes, "You cannot legislate morality." Something similar is true of enforcing openness to intellectual diversity—institutional policies have changed over the past forty years, but attitudes such as "my classroom, my way" still exist. Enforcing classroom support begins with the acceptance of intellectual diversity and attitude change, especially among those who teach and provide services and support.

WHAT *MIGHT* WORK?

Before investigating what might work, it is important to return briefly to the caution that "college is not for everyone." On the positive side, people do find happiness and success in life without a college degree—whether autistic or neurotypical, formal higher education is not everyone's best or only path. Furthermore, success in college for the autistic person depends on many things, including a frank and honest look at the difference between *neurodiversity* and *neurological disability*, two terms still debated in the overall discussion about autism and higher education.

Since the mid-2000s, these two terms have risen to prominence as students, families, and institutions consider the way forward. Both refer to neurology, but each speaks to a different aspect of diversity. Dana Lee Baker summarized this dichotomy by noting that *neurological disability* refers to the legal definition that a disability is anything that limits a "major life activity." This, in turn, is the result of how the individual experiencing the difference identifies him- or herself. Baker's research surveying families of children with autism suggests that when a student with a neurological disability comes to an institution of higher education, care must be taken to "navigate the sharpening divide between interests related to inclusion and those related to identity," (2006, p. 15).

In other words, when it comes to the "major life activity" at the core of this book—access to higher education—we can ask two questions. First: are accommodations chiefly about legally including autistics on an even playing field for higher education? Alternatively, will successful accommodations for students on the spectrum have to allow also for differences that flow from autistic identity? These two questions are at the crux of the conversation now taking place about autism and higher education. Put a different way, when it comes to the kinds of support offered by higher education institutions to students with an autistic identity, how must we design accommodations in order to maintain academic integrity, and how may accommodations be specified to support academic success without the student on the spectrum receiving unfair advantage?

Academic success in young adults with ASD is the result of a conflation of circumstances that include legal assumptions, situational expectations, and contextual conditions as well as diagnostic criteria. Most people would not be able to confront such a web of challenges as this and succeed, whether they had ASD or not. Several possible approaches to supporting students with ASD have emerged that can positively influence the success rate of college students on the spectrum.

Environmental "Safety"

The most fundamental approach involves making the postsecondary environment "safe" for people with intellectual differences. One aspect of safety is psychological; another is physical. Most quality K–12 schools systems now have an expectation for safety consciously built in. Administrators do not tolerate bullying. Many elementary classrooms now have a carefully planned sensory menu available, so it does not become too overwhelming for students on the spectrum who often suffer from sensory sensitivities. In fact, specialized classrooms that follow the TEACCH method specifically manipulate the environment in sensory-friendly ways to achieve goals for their students with ASD. (The TEACCH model originated at the University of North Carolina - Chapel Hill (UNC). This structured learning environment recognizes differences in rate and nature of development within and among children with ASD.) Unfortunately, as children grow into proto-adults in high school and postsecondary school, the amount of emphasis placed on safety diminishes. The assumption seems to be that the older students get, the more they *should* be able to protect themselves and find physical and psychological safety without assistance.

Clearly, this assumption—this "should"—is too absolute to be sustained. Bullying and hazing, physical, sexual, and verbal abuse, and just plain sensory overload do still exist on college campuses even among neurotypical students. College administrators deal with such serious matters each day, and many conscientious postsecondary-school public safety departments all over the country work hard to ensure that such tragedies on campus occur less and less often and that they are properly dealt with when they do. However, not all the effects of autism are so immediately dramatic. The small, everyday effects can build up and wreck a college career. Many strategies exist to assuage these effects as well.

The first thing that can be done is to educate a college's students, faculty, and staff about the effects of autism on campus, just as has been done for years with date rape and harassment. Such a media campaign could be part of a disability awareness month or autism awareness month promotional. Students generally listen better to other students, so including the voices of students with autism and Asperger's syndrome and their allies is important. Follow-up is also essential, and if there can be an academic tie-in such as a guest speaker or a class on autism and culture, you can build it into the campaign from the start. If promotion is successful, then a policy change may be next.

Policy changes do not have to wait on a dramatic incident to emerge. Discussions between and among neurotypicals and autistics—both faculty and students—can lead to a policy change; in fact, this book is an attempt to bring such discussions to the table. Policy changes also do not have to be overarching and brand new. They might involve something as simple as adding the words "intellectual differences," or "autism" or "Asperger's syndrome" to an already existing rule on inclusion in the code of conduct. For the most part, a college is, at its best, a confederation of like-minded adult learners who believe that the pursuit of truth is an end in itself, and can lead to a better world overall and more opportunity for those who wish to take part.

Such information campaigns and admirable goals hinge upon the basics: "Can the student follow his or her routine without being ostracized by dorm mates?" and "Are the lights too bright in the classroom?" Though an assumption is made again here that the students, being adults, will find ways to ask for what they need in such settings, students with intellectual differences may not always be aware or able to do so, especially when they first arrive in the new setting.

As a result, those students who choose to live at college should have resident assistants who know what autism is and how it may affect someone. In turn, the resident assistants should also be encouraged to make the necessary changes to ensure that students in their care feel comfortable enough with their living situation after hours that they can function academically during school hours. Remember: modifications (i.e., changes to the curriculum or the outcomes) are not legally mandated for adult learners; however, you can make modifications to residential halls and the system that regulates their use.

For instance, preferential housing does not have to be for seniors only. Perhaps a student with autism can receive his or her choice of a private room or a particular roommate even if he or she is only a freshman. Many postsecondary schools now have extensive "first-year programs" that serve the purpose of making the transition to college a supported experience with early and extensive orientation weeks, specified living units, and ready-made cohort groups, peer mentors, and academic advisors. These are all modifications to the usual approach, and though the verdict is out as to whether they actually help a person with "persistent deficits in social communication and social interaction across multiple contexts" (2013; 50). However, they must be done with autistic awareness in mind, students can approach their first year with more tools to address the challenges they find in their new residential setting.

For many students who do not receive the benefit of a first-year program or who do not choose to attend a residential college, challenges still remain with regard to their feeling of safety in the classroom. Addressing those challenges may be incumbent on the instructor in the setting, at least at the beginning of the semester or quarter, because the nature of autism makes it unlikely that the student will bring up the environmental issues within the classroom that could later cause problems, even if he or she knows that they exist. To make things more complicated, classrooms at many colleges are arbitrarily assigned, sometimes at the last minute, and professors seldom have the opportunity to prepare the space to suit their own purposes. So, one possible change that sensory-friendly institutions of higher education may want to implement is to review their procedures on room assignments and instructor influence over particular spaces on behalf of their students and their students' needs.

At any rate, an exercise to do in the classroom on the first day of classes (as though there is not already enough to do on the first day, I know) is included in the Appendix to mitigate issues that might arise later in the semester when they can cause even more frustration in a student (see p. 219). The design brings awareness of invisible differences to the entire classroom as well as lure out students who might have one.

Making the postsecondary setting feel "safe" psychologically and physically for all students is an ongoing challenge with its own rewards. It takes extra time, perhaps even time away from the meat of the subject of the class, but as many other institutions have learned, a little time and forethought now can improve the outcome later.

A woman told me a story about the difference between the birth experience she had with her first child and the one she had a decade later with the birth of her last child. The first delivery room was cold, technical, and full of tubes, raw aluminum bed rails, and half a dozen machines that all went "beep" in various discordant tones. The space she went to for her last delivery was warm, decorated in gentle colors, and the main visible piece of furniture in the room was a comfortable, specially designed birthing bed with a tranquil view of a springtime field out the window. "Of course, both kids turned out just fine," she told me. "But you know which birth experience I remember more completely, more fondly, more joyously...." Remembering what an instructor said in a classroom depends upon more than just oratorical finesse.

Contextual Reframing

A second approach to supporting students with ASD is called "contextual reframing" by Peter Vermeulen in his book *Autism as Context Blindness* (2012). In it, Vermeulen masterfully connects findings on context and brain science, perception, social interaction, communication, and knowledge schema to convince the reader that people with autism make meaning in ways that do not take into account the context. The word *context* comes with a long history of applications, beginning chiefly with its use in naming the "text around the text" as applied to Biblical and historical studies. The concept of context now extends into discussions about the meaning of art, music, politics, and history as well as the processing of thoughts, memories, and connections inside the human brain.

Vermeulen suggests that people with ASD process input from the bottom up, with less recognition and/or emphasis on what defines the information from the top down (although this processing may diminish with age and maturity). For instance, if given a complex painting of a scene with many components, a person with this kind of bottom-up "autistic cognition" would immediately set about taking in and evaluating each section of the artwork, whereas a person without autistic cognition might take in the whole scene based on his or her internal context of similar scenes with similar components. The person with autistic cognition would see the colors of the river, the man's hat, and the woman's blouse; the person without it would see a picnic and maybe even connect it to the history of French Impressionism that they learned at school.

Context blindness suggests that people with autistic cognition may make fixed one-to-one connections. People without autistic cognition do not do this; in fact, the common social language is often unfixed. Neurotypical people constantly make one-to-many connections based upon the context in which language occurs. Numerous examples of this exist in everything from the scientific literature to the depiction of autistic-like characters on TV and in the movies. In fact, one of the strengths of autism as context blindness is that the evidence for it is abundant and persistent—even across contexts, as the diagnosis states.

Autism as Context Blindness is, of course, much richer and more intriguing than described here, and is well worth a read. So how can an institution of higher education respond to its premises? Will it lead to support that works specifically for autistic students in ways that current accommodations and support do not?

Just as the approach we call environmental safety is mainly a matter of the providers being conscious of the *sensory* landscape of a classroom or other space on campus, so contextual reframing is a matter of faculty and staff being conscious of the *contextual* landscape surrounding their communications with autistic students. Indeed, an environment that is safe from a sensory point of view can be all that more autism friendly if it is also somewhere where communication is concrete and context clarified.

Concrete communication is one way of, as Vermeulen put it, "pressing the context button" (p. 360). In the cartoon *Dexter's Laboratory,* the genius main character has a sister named Dee Dee whose catchphrase is very relevant. Dee Dee often breaks into Dexter's secret lab and causes great chaos, and just before she does so, she usually says, "What does this button do?"

Before pressing the context button for our family, friends, and students on the spectrum, we first should find out more about what context is and what it does in a given situation. Vermeulen's well-researched working definition of context included both the environment outside our brains and the memories and hard-wired experiences inside them. Context may be immediate, close by, or far away; it may be significant or incidental. In every case, the most important aspect of context is that it influences how we *make meaning* from our everyday experiences. The ability to select elements in context that are useful and meaningful, and use them, is context sensitivity. The neurotypical human brain is, inherently, context sensitive (Vermeulen, 2012), and if the theory is correct, the autistic brain is *not* inherently so.

As is apparent from a look at the diagnosis chart given earlier, both criterion A and criterion B in the diagnosis of autism have some connection to "meaning-making" and to the challenges that human beings on the spectrum may have to aligning their form of meaning-making to that of other human beings around them. At the core of criterion A, "a persistent impairment in reciprocal social communications and social interaction," is the struggle to find the common ground necessary to share meaning with another person. Similarly, criterion B, "restricted, repetitive patterns of behavior, interests, or activities," revolves around the meaning for which a person chooses to use their attention, heart, intellect, and daily undertakings. Pressing the context button is one way of aligning our meaning-making with that of another person whose brain takes in and processes context differently from our own.

One can easily recognize this in an interaction between a neurotypical adult and a child with autism. When my grandchild's attention focuses on lining his Matchbox cars up along the edge of the bed, I can join him by noticing the meaning he is giving to the context of the cars and the bed: big red ones first, then little red ones. Next are the big blue ones, then the little blue ones, and so on. The real communication deficit is cleared away once I see how he is making meaning out of his activity, then I can join in by doing the same thing with, say, his toy airplanes. So I line up his toy airplanes by size and color along the side of his bed opposite the cars. An observer would call this "parallel play," but for us, it is also mutual meaning-making. I saw in his play how he was defining the context of our experience. He pressed my context button, and when I "get it," I can "fly in" two peanut butter sandwiches on his largest, green toy plane—and land it in its proper location, of course. With luck, I have pressed a different context button for him, one that says, "It's time for lunch." One thing is for sure, this never would have happened if I tried to take him away from his car arranging just because the clock said "12:09."

In an interaction between adults in a higher education setting, the context button may be harder to define and press. Autistics are sometimes described as "concrete thinkers," and the assumption with this is usually that concrete language is not as developmentally advanced, valuable, or beautiful, as figurative language. However, the difference between a lab write-up and an art history term paper is not always a matter of aesthetics. It may just be a matter of the professor making the context of the assignment clear and precise so students can understand and meet expectations. (For an example, see Chapter 10.)

Supported Self-Advocacy

A third approach to supporting students with autism gets at the core of this conundrum: you can lead a horse to water, but you can't make him drink. Put more pragmatically, transition professionals who guide students into postsecondary schools often suggest that they get involved with as many people, groups, clubs, and departments as possible. Yet after an introduction to autism as context blindness, they may find themselves wondering if sending a student who may be context insensitive into a sea of contrasting and maybe even competing contexts like college is really the best thing to do. Is it even fair? These are important and valuable questions, and what lies beneath is our approach to adolescence.

One of the hallmarks of adolescence in our society is that at a certain age, we encourage our young people to choose their own context (e.g., college, work, military) and learn how to thrive there. Tacitly this also means that they may choose to ignore some of the contexts in which they currently find themselves, in favor of others that they want to pursue. All of this encouragement hinges on the assumption that a person is aware enough of the postsecondary setting in which they will find themselves that they can ask for what they need once there. We call this "self-advocacy," from the word "advocate," which literally means to talk aloud or "to give voice to." Self-advocacy is a skill that all people must learn, and it usually begins in earnest at the same time a child becomes an independent adult. However, self-advocacy hinges upon the ability to understand the setting or context in which you find yourself at any given point in your life. A neurotypical person learns that you speak up for yourself with your dorm mate in a much different way than you do with your academic advisor. People with autism need support in these matters because they may not be using context to determine their course of action. The question is, how is that provided?

The first thing to say is that we *must* provide it. Self-advocacy always involves direct support, at least at first. For instance, the mother bird calls to the baby bird from just a few inches away when she is trying to get the little one to leave the nest. Once the fledgling is out, the mother bird calls from farther and farther across the field. Before the summer is very far advanced, the young birds are finding food, avoiding danger, and generally getting along. Yet a closer observation in my backyard often reveals that the parent bird is usually still nearby, especially keen to alerting their offspring of dangers that they may or may not yet be able to perceive. It is the same way with humans.

In general, self-advocacy and disclosure are not self-evident skills, to say the least. They involve complex issues related to communication, self-confidence, building alliances, and administrative policy-making. They may sometimes even involve the use of documentation such as the IEP or other medical/psychological evaluations and paperwork. A thorough exploration of all these areas would take several books, but one can make a start by looking at a couple of the sources now available on the subject. See the excellent and thought-provoking collection of essays entitled *Ask and Tell*, edited by Stephen Shore (2004), or one of the many guides on autism and adolescence, such as *Growing Up on the Spectrum* by Lynn Koegel and Claire LaZebnik (2009), or *Adolescents on the Autism Spectrum: A Parent's Guide* by Chantal Sicile-Kira (2006). Each of these sources assist parents, allies, or teens with autism, but once teens step up to college, self-advocacy moves from being merely an important skill to becoming *the* essential competency needed for success.

You can find many examples of supported self-advocacy in the college environment. They vary from one-time workshops for students identifying themselves as on the spectrum to the establishment of ongoing peer mentor relationships or academic coaches. Mentors or coaches also have a variety of ways to support the students:

1. Help the student set goals and prioritize them.
2. Assist the student with writing a script that includes what to say and who to say it to.
3. Think through cause and effects ahead of time, pressing the context button in the process.
4. Be present at key academic and other appointments.
5. Be willing to be absent and to fade support as the student gains confidence.
6. Debrief with the student after important self-advocacy events.

As noted in earlier chapters, the key elements to supported self-advocacy success are 1) student buy-in, and 2) consistent follow-up. Nothing will happen unless the student wants to participate in its happening. Additionally, though difficult financial decisions constantly challenge nearly all higher education institutions regarding how to use their resources, it may be a hard sell to provide the resources necessary for truly consistent follow-up. Still, intellectual differences are here to stay and it is extremely important to give them the attention and resources they need.

RESOLVING THE SOUND LAB CASE STUDY

The case study at the beginning of this chapter can be resolved by looking specifically at the three aspects of student support on campus: safety, reframing the context, and supported self-advocacy.

Environmental Safety in the Sound Lab

First, what can make the environment for the student safe? This one is trickier than usual because the degree this student is pursuing, Digital Design and Graphics (DDG), requires him to take an audio component, and some of the "sound effects" being manipulated in the lab may be too harsh for the hypersensitive student to stand. (Remember that in college, instructors cannot modify curriculum—although they must legally provide access to said curriculum for those with a disability). Knowing that the student has to take and pass this lab, several things were addressed.

The most obvious safety issue is the physical safety of the student. Loud, complex, and discordant sound could actually be painful for him, yet he did not initially know how to protect his ears from it. Once the professor understood this, he was able to provide safety with assistance. He allowed the student to use sound dampening earphones in the lab, and they could then use simple hand signals to communicate at each step in the teaching/learning process. Another idea was to provide solo time for the student in the lab so that he could accomplish his own work without the interference of other students' sounds. This sort of accommodation pushes the university and the teacher to consider unusual logistics like opening the lab and providing oversight of its expensive equipment during "off hours"; however, once this is put in place, other students who are not on the spectrum can also benefit.

Note: Sensory challenges in a student may be misunderstood or even masked as they move from the K–12 setting to the higher education setting. A student has to know what his or her sensory issues are and find ways to accommodate those needs in the higher education setting. All this has to happen before the student can communicate what he or she needs to faculty, friends, and staff. The student in the example already had an accommodation (ear plugs) that he used; however, for those who don't yet know how to describe or find solutions for sensory needs, a book like *Sensory Issues and High-Functioning Autism Spectrum and Related Disorders*, 2nd Edition (Myles, Cook, Miller, Rinner, & Robbins, 2012) provides a good start to address the issues.

Another logistics adjustment was necessary in order to provide the appropriate follow-up this student needed as well—namely, regular check-ins with the professor. These check-ins would allow a continual dialogue to form between the instructor and the student about the effects of the everyday, small sensory issues that the student is facing—sometimes not just in sound lab, but also in the other areas of his college life—dorms, dining halls, and even parties. Knowing how sound interacts with all aspects of life is at the heart of exploring sound for a career in DDG. What sounds startle everyone? What sounds bring calm to most? The student who lives out the answers to these kinds of questions will stand out in the industry. This may be one case where a "disability" associated with a spectrum disorder (sound sensitivity) becomes an asset. Putting time and effort into making sure that the physical safety of the environment comports with the student's needs could actually produce a better-equipped graduate.

Assuring the psychological safety of this student may lead to these positive outcomes. Initially using the cognitive map exercise or something like it could help every student in the class. Use of some kind of learning environment assessment and sharing exercise might also have helped the student and instructor avoid the pressing situation that initiated the problem described at the beginning of this chapter. The whole reason for spending time on classroom procedures during the first few days of the semester is to be proactive, not reactive. Yet just doing an exercise is not enough—follow-up is essential. Sometimes students on the spectrum do not share what their needs are; often, they may not yet know. So once the exercise is over, it is important to return occasionally to what the teacher and the students shared about their "ideal learning environment." Timing is important here. Returning to the results just before a particularly chaotic sonic lab session may perhaps be important.

Finally, when it comes to psychological safety in the classroom, it is best if the instructor does not invest in his or her own relevance, or even that of the subject they teach. Relevance occurs inside the student's mind, not on the instructor's lips. No matter how great or dismal an instructor may be, the student lives in an environment that feels either safe or unsafe. That environment forms the crucible on which he or she decides to be motivated or just to "get by." The only way to influence this is for the instructor to check in regularly with the students (and not just on an exam) to see if what is being taught is getting across. If it is not, then he or she needs to find out what is getting in the way of learning. This is the best way to make motivated students, inherently interesting lessons, and ultimately, prepared job seekers (for those going into the field of endeavor, whatever field that is).

Framing the Context: Highly-Charged Language in the Sound Lab

Before returning to the sound lab example, here is another story from a different angle:

> Halfway through the semester a student came to his advisor and said that he was shifting his major from Associate of Science to Culinary Arts. Being a good advisor, he asked the student a couple of questions as he prepared to make the change on the student's file. He soon learned that the student wanted to be a chef because he "liked to cook at home." After a few minutes more, he also learned that the student had concerns about the change.
>
> "I've been downstairs to the kitchen lab, and it is kind of hot in there. Also, I really don't want to get burned." The advisor listened respectfully to the student and tried not to say aloud what kept coming to his mind: "If you can't stand the heat..." (don't go into culinary arts).

Helping a student on the autism spectrum "press the context button" or frame the context of his or her choices is not always easy. Sometimes what any 18- to 22-year-old imagines for their future is fraught with "red flags" for an adult ally. Part of the ally's response is not to run down the student's dream based on his or her own impressions. At the same time, the ally is also there to help the student do a reality check in order to pursue another dream that fits them better, if necessary. There are a number of viable ways to do this.

Start with a visual—an upside-down triangle. In the case of the student in the chef illustration, have them put "become a chef" across the long top line. It can help if they are encouraged to elaborate on just what they mean by "chef."

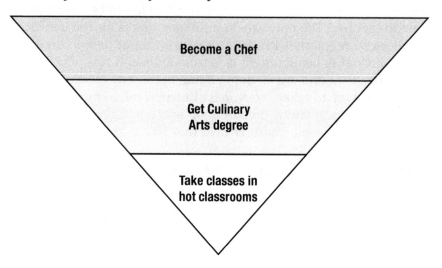

Then, help them put in the other steps that they will have to take before they get to the goal. As they get closer to the lowest point of the triangle, encourage them to be more and more specific. What immediate thing(s) are they being asked to do? Many of the immediate steps will not be academic. In the case of a culinary understudy, it means taking a class that meets in a very hot classroom.

It does not take long before the student will begin to draw the lines from the point of the triangle where they are now to the goal line. Questions like, "Will you be asked to do tasks in this environment throughout your career as a _____?" can help the student begin to frame the context. This is one way of pushing the context button that does not allow students to become too over-focused on outcome OR on immediate (sometimes, onerous) tasks. With a careful application of pace and lead questioning, using the triangle can even help the student make meaning of their dreams and aspirations. It also helps a student rehearse ways to communicate those dreams and aspirations. In one sweep, it addresses issues raised by both aspects of the autism diagnosis—flexibility and communication—which is, after all, the goal of pressing the context button.

Contextual reframing does not have to dwell on just the grand questions of life, like what I will do for a living. It also can allow a student to deal with smaller things like the use of language in the classroom. For instance, it soon became clear that there were ways in which he could press the context button in the sound lab. For example, the student in the sound lab had often used the phrase, "I feel like I'm going to hit someone," even though, as the coach pointed out, he had not actually hit anyone since seventh grade. He said this to his mother at home and even to his friends while at the Student Union; however, the phrase is an example of "highly-charged language" when it is said in class. The student code of conduct required the professor to take action because others may consider the phrase threatening.

In order to help the student discover the context, he and his support team created the following chart, which the student filled out (Fig. 6.1).

FIG. 6.1   Highly-Charged Phrase: *I Feel Like I'm Going to Hit Someone*

Example in Context	Why a Student Might Use It	What It Means in Context	What Can Happen as a Result	Alternative
Lab—Too much noise	Hypersensitive to sound	Code of Conduct E4a (p. 51) Threatening: implying or causing physical harm…	Professor HAS to take action: separate student, call Public Safety	Keep it to yourself or say "It is too noisy in here; I need to step out."
At lunch in the student union—too much noise	Hypersensitive to sound	"This place is noisy! I can't eat lunch here."	Friends leave with you or you go alone	Say, "Let's go to a quieter place for lunch" instead of the highly charged phrase.
*These tables are also available in the Appendix.				

It is worth noting here that this student had memorized much of the student code of conduct during his two-week autism-student cohort orientation to college. However, he did not discover the "charge" that certain words take on inside the classroom setting until the professor, his academic coach, and his mother helped him see the context. When he and his allies realized this, they decided to come up with the a table (Fig. 6.2) to help other autistics grasp what inadvertently happened to him.

The chart starts with the E4 codes of the student code of conduct since those most often trip up students on the spectrum at this college. The assumption is that students could memorize these regulations but still misunderstand them, just like what happened to the student in the sound lab.

All of this can be reactive with a specific student in a specific context by a coach or teacher. It also may be proactive, completed by student, allies, instructors, and staff to think through what might happen ahead of time. This in turn might allow a student to think through his or her favorite phrases with context in mind before they actually blurt them out and possibly get in trouble.

Pushing the "context button" can happen in many ways—both formal ways like the use of this chart, and informal ways, by gently and surreptitiously reminding a student whose words are commandeering a lecture that they are in a classroom, where everyone gets a turn to speak. The key is to make the context, often unconsciously understood by neurotypicals, concrete and clear to those with autistic cognition.

Supported Self-Advocacy and Helicopter Parents

The DDG student in the case study had already worked hard on self-advocacy when he found himself in his negative situation. He had come to school as part of an autism-specific cohort and gone through two weeks of extensive orientation. He listened to his coach well for nearly two years, visited each of his professors two or three times during the semester, filed for and received accommodations through the campus disability services provider, attended classes, sought tutoring and academic help, used an assignment schedule, and took an active role in the campus Autism Acceptance club. Despite all this, he still ran into an issue directly related to the way autism affected him. What does this say about the situation vis-à-vis autism and higher education on his campus?

Two things. The first is that plenty of room still remains to find best practices and supports for autism in college settings, even on progressive campuses among well-informed students with autism. Disability providers, even at their best, need more experience finding accommodations that fit their autistic students' needs. Professors, tutors, and staff can still train in and share best practices. Students must still be the ones who primarily embrace the responsibility for executive functioning and seek support when

FIG. 6.2 "Highly-Charged Language" (Based on E4 of the Code of Conduct, XYZ University)

If you use the words: "threaten," "intimidate," "harass," "haze," or "stalking" from the Code of Conduct, be sure that you understand the highly charged nature of the word in different contexts. Follow-up and legal interdiction is REQUIRED once certain words or phrases come out of your mouth. So, use them wisely.

Look at the chart below and weigh the situations, then come up with an alternative.

"Highly Charged" Phrase	Context(s) (Change the contexts)	Why a Student Might Use It	What It Means in Code of Conduct	What Can Happen as a Result	Alternative
I really think that you should loan me your calculator for the weekend. (said 20 times)	Fellow student keeps saying this over and over	Don't have money for their own calculator	E4b (p.51) Intimidation— pressuring another unreasonably	Charges can be filed by receiving student; loss of friendship; calculator gone	
Don't let her sit here with us in the lounge; She totally has ASS-bergers.	Joke among friends in the gaming clan	Trying to make friends, be funny	E4c (p. 51) Discriminatory Harassment— speech or conduct depriving access, enjoyment, benefits to campus	Loss of friendship; hurt feelings; isolation; charges filed	
If you want to hang out with us, you have to drink this concoction—all of us did it.	Club rule or group pressure when you come to your first club meeting	Trying to prove him- or herself to others	E4d (p. 51) Hazing— endangering behavior as a condition for affiliation	Physical illness; unnecessary pain or humiliation; charges filed	
Saying: "This guy is stalking me" to a faculty member or a Public Safety officer walking by.	Student's behavior is annoying you, and he or she won't let up after being asked to	Feels annoyed or wants to get his or her friend in trouble	E4e (p. 51) Stalking— repetitive menacing pursuit interfering with peace and safety	Campus employee MUST report this to authorities	

they need it; however, they do not have to do this alone. Success for a student on the spectrum comes from an institution-wide commitment to doing "learning" in a dynamic, multifaceted way. Take the DDG student, for instance. Without the work he did with his coach and his early-look program, he would not have made it to his second year, let alone the sound lab where things got tricky for a while.

Without the professor taking the extra time to assure that the physical and psychological environment of the lab was safe for all, including the student with autism, the incident might have ended with the student's expulsion based on a violation of the student code of conduct.

Without the acceptance and understanding of the autistic student's fellow students (something not mentioned in this chapter), reactionary rejection, doubt, and suspicion might have ruled the day, instead of patience and acceptance of intellectual processing differences.

Finally, without the student's mother stepping into the resolution, who may know the student better than anyone else, the truth might never have come out. Her summation of the entire incident was this: "The words he chose to say were at the heart of the problem, not what he actually did." This allowed the team, including the student, to have the insight they needed to move through and past the incident.

In nearly thirty years of work in the field of special education, the cry against "helicopter parents" has often gone up. To be sure, the balance between hanging on and letting go is very important to the healthy development of all of us, but as one colleague put it after she heard of the resolution to this case study: "They may be 'helicopter parents,' but they still can get you off the ground."

CHANGE

At the beginning of the chapter, I mention this question: What supports might be offered that explicitly address the effects of ASD? Coming up with specific and effective accommodations directly related to the effects of autism at your institution of higher learning is probably still a work in progress. In order for them to move out of the theoretical stage, students and staff can look into the areas of Environmental Safety, Contextual Reframing, and

Supported Self-Advocacy to design and implement approaches that work. We can do this work right now, even though knowledge concerning the effects of autism on postsecondary schools is still inadequate.

Despite the blind spot in our understanding of autism's effects on people and institutions, there has been a noticeable change in the experiences of parents and students entering academia. For instance, in the mid-2000s, a student with autism who was considering coming to college might have found and looked over a disability office's brochure and reached the conclusion that they offered him no accommodations that would fit his needs; therefore, there was no reason to self-disclose his or her diagnosis.

Now, that same student might find, with a little probing, several institutions with a better sense of how to support autistic students. There is a kind of grass-roots movement among small, one-person disability services offices—and some larger disability services departments—to approach autism consciously, in a unique and different way. Many residential schools, for instance, at minimum have established autism-friendly dorms. Some have established formal guidelines or principles to inform their faculty and staff of the burgeoning needs associated with the effects of autism on their campus (like Toledo University and Bowling Green), several have designed courses and even programs about autism (like Wisconsin Tech), and most have increased the awareness of autism's effects on their campus. Enough of a movement exists now that this is a common story shared among friends and allies of college freshmen:

 ANONYMOUS

"I've got a great story to tell you about my daughter in college. Last week, she took a list of three accommodations to her professors that she and the Accessibility Office had developed. Two of them agreed to provide the support, and only one refused, saying that it just did not 'fit his lecture style!'" The mom was very proud and excited as she finished, "Yesterday, the Accessibility Office emailed the disagreeable professor to see if he can work it out with her, and they even copied our daughter."

QUESTIONS

1. What makes a campus feel "safe" to a person whose social approach at a faculty/student mixer may be less than adequate for the task? Is just recognizing that such an event makes for great anxiety in some people enough, or is it important to carry that knowledge over into a faculty or staff meeting where such events are being planned? How might this be done at your institution? How would knowing this change the way in which one-on-one student–instructor meetings were held?

2. What specific ways can neurotypical and autistic staff and faculty make context more conscious to those for whom understanding context is not conscious or easy?

3. Work together to make your own list of things that can be done in a living unit or on the first day of classes to make the environment feel "safe" for students with autism.

4. Use the chart on page 101 and come up with alternatives to each scenario row.

5. If you are a professor, brainstorm two or three ways in which you could bring context framing into the curriculum of your favorite class, then run those past the autistics in your group. Bear in mind two principle questions: How must accommodations be designed in order to maintain academic integrity, and how may accommodations be specified to support academic success without the student on the spectrum receiving unfair advantage?

6. Broadly speaking, the planting and supplanting of context has been at the root of all of Western intellectual history. The ideas of those thinkers who rose to a position of prominence defined the context of the university (and thus, the "universe"). Those who did not understand, even grapple, with that context were lost to history, and those whose

context supplanted the old worldview took over. Think of Galileo and the Church, of Einstein and time. Don't discuss the popular question: "Were these greats autistic?" Instead, discuss how their form of cognition helped and hindered the new contexts they generated.

7. If your group is not afraid of a really hot topic, discuss the degree to which parents of college-age students with autism ought to be involved with their educational and life choices.

8. To what degree have you seen your institution change for the better in regard to offering access to education for students with autism over the past 10 years?

Two Models

Intake and Orientation

E very higher education institution has a mission. Whether you look at it from a humanistic standpoint or a business one, that mission is to develop a cadre of allies—faculty, staff, and students—who can connect to address the inspiration and challenge of welcoming and counting intellectually-diverse people among their numbers. Models and systems for doing this are growing, but they all begin with just a few motivated folks, or maybe even with just one frustrated person.

Becoming Allies, or "How to Obtain Support in College and Still Look Cool"

My name is Wade. The day I came in for my admissions interview, I was sure I was ready for college. I had been to the bookstore. I had been to the cafeteria with my sister. I had been to seven inter-collegiate sports activities at "XXU." I did well in high school with only a little help for math. I was sure I was ready for college, as I said. But once Mr. Smith started telling me how hard it was going to be to find time to study and make all the appointments I needed to make, I wasn't so sure anymore.

That's where the real "fun" began. I nearly lost it when my online registration did not go through, and there was a huge line down the hall to get to the registrar's window. A couple of days later I decided to go back to Mr. Smith and tell him that I had Asperger's syndrome. He helped me set up an interview with the advocate at the Disability Services department. I don't like the name "disability," but I was fine with the woman I met.

She told me about a two- to three-hour-long orientation option they have for autistics like me. She also mentioned a longer program that would follow me for the first year of classes. As she talked, I remembered how I heard that Aspies like me (I do like that name) are not supposed to care about looking cool—but I do anyway. Turns out there are over fifty kids on campus with Asperger's syndrome or high-functioning autism, and some of them have the same concerns I do: "How will I fit in here?" and "Am I ready for college?"

TRANSITION TO COLLEGE: TWO MODELS

When any student on the spectrum comes to college, one question is on his or her mind—"How will I know if I am ready?" The short answer is, "You're not ready until you take into account how ASD affects you academically." In order to learn that, the student must find allies to help him or her discover what their academic skills and challenges are. Many models for doing this are emerging at two- and four-year schools every year. This chapter presents two such models. The first approach begins at intake and provides a seminar specifically designed for students with autism. The second uses a three-part curriculum that begins with students before classes start and follows them through their entire first year of college.

Before anything is accomplished, two simultaneous actions may occur. First, a student has to decide to find support on campus; at the same time, the campus has to equip its faculty and staff with programs, tools, and attitudes that allow them to become autism allies. In other words, success in higher education begins when students like Wade decide to turn their frustration into reasoned and thoughtful self-disclosure and faculty like Mr. Smith have tools at their disposal to offer autistic students, and along with the expertise and interest to help the system work for students who self-disclose.

One of the two models that follow depends upon the resources of the academic institution and the needs of its student population. Both models come from a similar background approach and each utilize data-gathering tools. The difference between the two is chiefly a matter of how the institution administers support. Both begin with a vision and some data gathering.

Beginning with the End in Mind

When the team to support autistic students first sat down to decide how to begin our program, they asked, "What adjective(s) will describe a successful student emerging from this program?" The adjectives they decided on were "independent" and "confident." In order to develop a program they hoped would produce students like this, they came up with nine "criteria for success." The outcome they had in mind: at the end of the one-year program, the student will function independently and feel confident in all nine areas. You can see from Figure 7.1 on the following page that in order to teach toward independence, both the student and the faculty member in charge of the program share responsibility for accomplishing the goals in each criterion.

Criteria that require greater support early in the year lessen later in the year as the faculty person fades. For instance, if a student requested that the program advocate be present as she met with her professor on week one of the semester, then by week three of the semester, all parties understand that the advocate will only be involved, for example, by helping her write a script beforehand, but not by being present. By the end of the first year, the student would do all the work before, during, and after meeting with her professor, utilizing the program advocate only as a resource, or to help debrief from the meeting.

In order to ascertain the confidence level of the student, a self-reported college confidence questionnaire using a Likert scale and based on the nine criteria for success is given to each student three times during the program year. A copy of this simple self-report may be found in the Appendix.

Looking back at the results from this tool, some interesting outcomes appear. Each class and cohort shows an overall increase in confidence across the year—giving the team confidence that the program works and the students meet the criteria. However, some criteria for individual students occasionally decrease. When this occurs, it seems to show that students' confidence can vary as they

FIG. 7.1 **Student's Criteria for Success: Student Responsibility and Allied Supports**

Category	#	Student Criteria for Success	Student's Responsibility	Program's Consultative Supports
INDEPENDENCE	1	Access Office of Disability Services *Appointment Checklist*	Make and keep appointment and follow through	Assist in paperwork, introductions/implementation of services; monitor ongoing academic challenges
	2	Independently schedule classes *Independent Registration*	Utilize advising services effectively; learn how to use website to get information; register and choose courses and major	Provide coaching and connections on registration, advising, and classes with fading support
	3	Independently transport self to/from campus and around campus locations *Year-end Attendance*	Follow instructions and/or lessons on accessing buildings and transportation	Provide transition services regarding transportation options
SOCIAL COMPETENCY	4	Negotiate peer and student–instructor relationships *Student–Instructor and Appointment Checklist*	Attend modules, make and keep appointments with instructors	Teach social skills modules; academic mediation; raise faculty awareness and provide faculty instruction on autism
	5	Participate in at least two nonacademic activities or events *Checklist with Comments*	Attend and write-up at least two nonacademic activities or events	Provide connections and information on campus events and clubs; encourage attendance and involvement

	6	Understand/follow Code of Conduct ***Completion of Instruction*** ***No Disciplinary Actions***	Attend, learn, and pass module on the Code of Conduct (85% or better)	Teach module on Code of Conduct; monitor behavior issues if they arise; mediate with Public Safety if needed
FUTURE PLANNING	7	Identify goals and develop a plan to reach them ***Student Future Plan***	Attend modules and transition meetings; interact with Campus Transition Resources	Provide transition coaching on employment, life planning skills, future plans
	8	Choose a program of study; achieve passing grades ***GPA 2.0 or better on Transcript***	Organize study plan and follow it; attend all classes; self-advocate; use writing and math labs; do your best; choose major by end of spring semester	Teach and monitor college skills, time management, organization; coach on how to find and interact with services on campus
	9	Increase self-awareness and knowledge of autism ***Complete Autism Project***	Complete final project, readings	Direct project and readings and monitor and refer as needed

discover just how college really works and learn to let go of how they thought it should work.

For instance, one student whose college confidence rating went up on eight of nine criteria but down on criterion number three explains:

> When I started, I thought that talking to college professors would be hard, but not any different really for me than talking to my old high school teachers. But after that first meeting with my chemistry professor, I discovered that I have to be way more organized when I knock on that door—they don't have as much time for me, and I have to come straight to the point.

The snapshot of any person's confidence on any given day is seldom consistent. Therefore, in order to be sure that the confidence and independence curves continue to bend upward for every student in a program, the students themselves have to know just how autism affects them as students and as people. This requires some hard data and a solid baseline from which to begin.

Data-Gathering Tools

I do not mean for the data-gathering tools and evaluations presented in this section to take the place of a thorough diagnostic test run by a licensed psychologist. Multi-reporting systems such as the Behavior Rating Inventory of Executive Functioning (Gioia, Isquith, Guy, & Kenworthy, 2000) and the Behavior Assessment for Children (Reynolds & Kamphaus, 2004) are common measures that often contribute to an autism diagnosis and should be considered when working with a student on the spectrum. The tools presented below are specific ways to help students pinpoint their needs as they approach the first day of college.

Just as both models presented here use the nine criteria for success as their foundation, they also utilize data-gathering tools to help a student gain insight into how autism affects their academic skills. The Autism View Rating (AVR) described in the beginning of this book is a great way to gain a snapshot of a student prior to their arrival on campus. Once they have started, the coach can use several other instruments.

Data-Gathering Tool	Authors	How to Use It	Strengths	Ways to Improve Functionality of Tool
My Areas of Difficulty Checklist	Wolf, Brown, & Bork (2009)	To elucidate goals for student to work on in one-on-one sessions	Covers several college-specific categories	May need more individualizing per student concerns
Social Skills Menu	Jed Baker (2005)	To tally concerns from entire group for plenary work	Detailed and orderly list of social skills	Contextualize for the college setting
Ziggurat Model—Underlying Characteristics Checklist—Self-Report (18 years and older)	Aspy & Grossman, (2015)	To gather data on strengths and needs related to the underlying autism	Extensive and thorough multiview	
College Survival and Success Scale	Liptak (2011)	Used as prescreen during Orientation Week	Young-adult specific	Adapt design for concerns of autistic students

The first one included here is a version of the My Areas of Difficulty Checklist taken from Appendix C of Wolf, Brown, and Bork's (2009) *Students with Asperger Syndrome*. As with Baker's (2005) Social Skills Menu, this checklist is an excellent way to align program curricula with the self-identified needs of the student.

More formal data-gathering tools may also be useful for setting up a program for autistics. One of these is the Underlying Characteristics Checklist—Adult Self-Report (Aspy & Grossman, 2007). Another is the College Survival and Success Scale (Liptak, 2011), which though not specifically designed for students with autism, yields valuable insights. No matter how you gather data, in order to contribute to student success, two things must happen. First, students need to understand the implications of what they discover. Second, the program must use that information consistently to teach toward a positive outcome.

If we think about students like Wade or Eric, we can see the importance of starting the first year of college well before the first day of classes. Students like these have decided to accept the role of autism in their decision to go to college. The students' K–12 allies have provided a snapshot through the AVR system or another baseline-generating tool. The students have made the decision to go to higher education allies and thoughtfully self-disclose to them. The school has adapted the criteria of success and provided a set of data-gathering instruments for the students to fill out. Everything is on the table for them to get the support they need to succeed. Now, what format will the support take? (Table detailing the components of both campus support models are available in the Appendix.)

Model One: Intake Interview and Follow-Up Workshop

One form of support on campus is an interview process specialized for students with autism, followed by a two- to three-hour follow-up workshop. As you can see on the sample "Intake Project Proposal" that follows, the goal of this approach is to provide a unified way to recruit, do the intake interview, identify individual needs, and support autistic students in their first term of college.

Intake Project Proposal

1. Students who identify themselves to a Disability Advocate are asked if they wish to participate in a two- to three-hour orientation designed to help them understand the challenges that ASD may present for them as a college student, and guide them toward support.

2. If they say "yes," then they receive information, a date, and a time. If "no," do nothing more.

3. If "yes," students receive the My Areas of Difficulty Checklist during the interview.

4. Complete the interview, hand out flyers, and set up reminder emails.

Prior to the workshop, the moderator collects and assesses the data from all workshop participants, and the topics for orientation are determined. Areas of instruction may include, but are not limited to, the categories on the data instrument: Learning and Memory, Attention and Organization, Communication, Behavior, Interpersonal, Sensory, Emotions, and Campus Resource Needs.

For example, three students signed up for a summer workshop. When their responses were tallied, all three participants chose these areas of concern: "I only like to study things that interest me"; "I don't have good study habits"; "I have trouble getting started on things"; I never plan my work in advance"; and "I only like to do one thing at a time." None of the other choices received checks from all three participants, although many choices received one or two checks. A few choices received no checks at all.

Topics

Because the first two most commonly-chosen areas of concern are from the category Learning and Memory, and the next three are from the category Attention and Organization, it becomes relatively easy to shape the topics for the workshop. In the example, spend thirty minutes on learning and memory issues, and thirty minutes on challenges the students face regarding attention and organization difficulties, and the supports on campus that can help them. Using the My Areas of Difficulty Checklist as a way to narrow the number of topics for a workshop is helpful, but it is important to not let go of the other presenting issues that participants bring. To this end, a well-prepared workshop will contain a folio on each of these suggested topics:

1. When I explain my ASD and ask for support, I . . .
2. When I manage my time, I . . .
3. When I am in class, I . . .
4. When I study, I . . .
5. When I have sensory issues on campus, I . . .
6. When I socialize or talk to peers, I . . .

That way, the instructor can cover all the bases and still highlight the areas that are particularly relevant to the entire participating group. Such administrative preparation will also make it possible to give this workshop several times each semester in order to accommodate varying student schedules and needs. Built into the model is a way of assessing its results. The moderator can track internal outcomes using a pretest before and posttest after the workshop based on the checklist. Once students are in the workshop setting, they can be encouraged to set up follow-up appointments with other college personnel. With student permission, create a list-serve of emails to make sure that all the students in the workshop receive information on future autism-related events or programs. This group of emails can also be used to set up a student-led organization or "Autism Club" if the students seem interested.

Advantages and Disadvantages

The main advantage of the workshop model is that it provides the opportunity for Admissions or Disability Advocates to have a response immediately ready when a student self-discloses in the intake interview. Second, the model addresses several autism-specific challenges such as sensory issues and socialization concerns. A third advantage is that it requires minimal commitment from the student up front, although to make it work, the student must find ways to continue to work on the challenge areas that he or she discovers. Finally, it can be cooperative among several traditionally separated departments. Staffing and expertise for a program like this can logically come from Student Life, Advising, Developmental Education, or Admissions. It does not have to rely only on one department to be effective.

This model also has some disadvantages. Chief among them is that its success relies on making students aware of the workshop and getting them to participate in it. The foundation of this challenge takes us right back to developmental psychology. Many students simply do not want to think of themselves as needing support, especially early on in their college career. The attitude may be, "I don't need this now. Maybe later." Sometimes "later" happens after a student's grade point average drops; sometimes, "later" never arrives.

Another related disadvantage is that it is usually difficult to establish a consistent student–staff connection in a single two- to three-hour encounter. Even when a student does attend a workshop, it is still essential that the student and leader of the workshop create a working relationship in order to address how to apply what they learned in the "real world" of the classroom. An effective workshop structure contains an opportunity for feedback and follow-up.

For most students, whether neurotypical or on the spectrum, learning college success skills requires time. A two-hour workshop is a worthy project, but a program that covers at least a semester will yield better results. The second model is a one-year program that seeks to address the possible shortcomings of the workshop approach.

Model Two: Orientation Week, Coaching, and Plenary

The second model also uses the same data-gathering system as the workshop model, but stretched out over the entire first year of college, with three main components. The first component is a seven- to ten-day-long intensive orientation known as "Orientation Week." The second component consists of weekly, individualized coaching sessions. The third component is a weekly group discovery session or "plenary" group.

Intensive Orientation or "Orientation Week"

A sample schedule for an intensive orientation (Fig. 7.3), or "Orientation Week," is on the following page. (A copy is also available in the Appendix.) This time occurs before the beginning of classes. If an institution already has a pre-class orientation for its incoming freshman, the time devoted to Orientation Week activities for students with autism will be affected, but can still be worked in. The purpose of this time is beginning to establish the new routine of college.

If the student comes with his or her own routine, this also can be linked to the Orientation Week itinerary. For instance, one student came with a well-established morning routine that ended with him adjusting his shoelaces just outside his front door each morning before he went to school. After some thought and persuasion, he agreed to move this final step of his routine from his front door to the classroom so that at 8:50, just before the Orientation Week sessions started for the day, he would adjust his shoelaces inside the classroom where the group was about to meet. This allowed him to be on time and ready to fulfill the expectation that all students in the program would meet from 9:00 to 3:00 each day of Orientation Week.

Time and timing is often a very important piece of a student with autism's unique approach to life. Establishing a new routine in the form of Orientation Week to replace older routines lays the groundwork for how to complete schedules once classes start (see Chapter 3). Orientation Week is designed to introduce some of the expectations of college to the student gently prior to the presence of any real consequences. Some of the expectations introduced include being on time, monitoring class participation, modeling interactive behaviors, and assigning and completing homework.

Each day of Orientation Week has several parts related to academia, and introduces social concepts as well. For instance, a

FIG. 7.3 Sample Orientation Week Schedule

	M 12th (1)	T 13th (2)	W 14th (3)	H 15th (4)	F 16th (5)	M 19th (6)	T 20th (7)
9:00	Intros & Photos CR	"Helping Students With Autism" (Brown)	The "How Will I Know?" (Wilson)	Circles Exercise (Wilson)	IS How to Get Good Grades	Social Skills Menu (Baker)	TS College Success Assessment
9:30	IS College Confidence Survey	DA Disability Services Overview	IS Getting Organized	TS Disability Disclosure		AV Advising	IS & Profs. "From My Point of View"
10:00	IS Student Criteria for Success	Former Student Q&A					
10:30		IS Code of Conduct 1					
11:00	MW Wright State Video		IS Code of Conduct 2 Quiz	IS & TS Scripts		IS Student Activities	BM National Science Foundation Grants
11:30			Lt. DB Public Safety	IS Transportation Issues	IS List of Questions		IS College Confidence Survey

12:00	Lunch	Lunch	Lunch	Lunch	Lunch	Lunch	Lunch
1:00	Personality Self-Score (Serebriakoff)	IS Learning styles	DF Working while a student	Campus Treasure Hunt	Library Tour Rm 302	Staff appts	Staff appts
1:30				Bookstore Pay Fees	1:1 with **IS** & **TS**	→	→
2:30	Walk thru classes, buildings, offices			Make ID		→	→
HW	Go over checklist for Orientation Week	Study for C of C quiz	Prioritize week 1–2	Skim booklets for "How to get good grades"	Go over Au 11 Checklist	Put appts on calendar	Complete checklists/ calendar

AV: Academic Advisor

DA: Disability Services Advocate

IS: Intervention Specialist or College Disability Advocate

TS: Transition Specialist or College Admissions/First Year Advocate data-gathering component or assessment occurs each morning. The students are given many of these tools so that they can begin to grasp aspects of their learning styles or personality preferences. After the data gathering, the day consists of academic modules based on the nine criteria for success, guest speakers from the college and the community, videos, group and individual exercises, afternoon field trips around campus, and the arrangement and follow-through of appointments with key professionals on campus.

Social components woven in throughout the day take the form of group exercises followed by analysis. This allows coaches and students alike to begin to understand the role of social/emotional intellect in college success. Additionally, it is encouraged that students go to lunch together—at first with the coach or a guest speaker and later in small groups of their own. Even this time is subject to gentle analysis. Some of the best early conversations within a cohort start with the question posed at 1:00 p.m.: "How did lunch go?" It is quite possible that a student needs some "alone time" at lunch. When that is the case, just remember that choosing what to do at lunch provides some autonomy for the individual student, related to his or her sensory and social needs.

Orientation Week is a "mini" college experience, but real college requirements can be done during each day. Organizers should alert administrative offices of the college that students from the program might be coming around to make student IDs and pay bookstore or class fees. Students may also visit their assigned classrooms and meet with advisors, tutors, faculty, or related staff if they are available. This is a great time for students to establish their accommodations at the college disability services department.

In short, Orientation Week is a time for the supportive allies on a campus to have the leisure and focus to help the incoming intellectually-diverse students succeed in their first encounters with university officials and procedures. To this end, those organizing the Orientation Week can ensure that students and parents have the correct paperwork in place prior to their meetings with disability and advising advocates. They can make sure that doors are open to the classrooms where students will learn and offices students will need to work with. A well-organized and thought-out intensive Orientation Week makes it easier to address sensory issues that might arise later and work through other issues that might lead to anxiety once classes start.

Weekly Academic Coaching

The second component of model two consists of weekly coaching sessions. These hour-long sessions are where ally and student can be the most individualized in their approach to college success. Unlike the workshop model, the one-year model can address many more challenges the students have self-identified. Figure 7.4 shows an example of the topics one student chose to address in these sessions:

FIG. 7.4   Topic Choice Sample Made by One Student

Learning and Memory
I have difficulty remembering instructions unless I write them down
I get overwhelmed in class or when studying
Sometimes my mind goes blank during exams
Campus Resources Needs
I don't have a quiet place to study
Attention and Organization
Sometimes I can't concentrate
Little things get me distracted
I need to move around when I have to sit still
I only like to do one thing at a time
Communication Skills
It is hard to listen to and understand people
I only talk about things that interest me
It is hard for me to start and join a conversation
Interpersonal Skills
Making friends seems really difficult to me
It is difficult for me to ask for help
All the activity in school gets me too stimulated
Emotions
People tell me I overreact to little things
Sensory
I get lost and don't remember how to get around places
I get stressed in noisy places
Note: This list comes from a modified version of Wolf, Brown and Bork's (2009) My Areas of Difficulty Checklist. Coaches, staff, and students can create their own such checklists based on the community in which they go to school.

Although these items came from a modified version of an existing data tool, anything that students identify as an area of growth for themselves can fit into a session. Furthermore, as students proceed through their first year of college, some items they checked originally will prove not as important as they once believed, and the need to work on other items may take precedent. Consider this conversation during a coaching session at the end of a student's first semester, halfway through the program:

Coach to A: I was looking at my notes from August before you came in today. Did you realize that you checked twenty-seven areas of difficulty on the checklist back then?

A to Coach *(with a very rare smile)*: Yes. There are only sixty-five or so to start with, but now I only have eight left that I would check.

Coach to A: After just half a year, you only have eight areas left. That is fantastic!

A to Coach: Really just nine, Coach, because I found a new one that wasn't on the list. Now that I have this new friend on campus, I want to figure out how to keep her around. Any ideas?

Ideally, the professional should drive the agenda of the individual sessions early on, and the student should drive the agenda later; however, the exact week that this turns over depends on the needs of the student. A coach can best prepare for this by providing options throughout the year, especially at the point when the student seems most ready to take over.

The coaching sessions move from a focus on understanding each class syllabus and creating a weekly schedule, to scripting and arranging an initial meeting with each professor. After that, the focus continues to be on weekly scheduling; weekly grade checks are added, and students are coached through how to meet midterm expectations by the due date. The second half of the first semester is the same: scheduling, checking in on assignments, and preparing projects and papers by their due dates. This is the ideal sweep of coaching sessions during the first semester, but things never run this smoothly for either the student or the coach. Inevitably anxieties arise—either academic or social, counterproductive habits are formed, and frustrations flare up.

When students have these challenges, it sometimes results in communication problems between the student and coach. The problem can take the form of a student "shutdown." Slumping in the chair, spacing out, closing off the input—especially verbal—are three signs that this may be going on in a one-on-one session. Two techniques can help get coach and student past this.

First, sometimes agreeing on the use of simple signs can help. For instance, one student whose processing slowed down when he experienced stress learned the sign for "slow." Way before the first incident of shutdown, the student, his coach, and even his professors all learned the sign together. The student would surreptitiously make the sign when he felt that he was about to go into overload and turn off. The professor agreed to do his best to slow down or repeat what had just been said when he saw the student making that sign. Other forms of body language can be used, too. The key is for all parties involved in communication to agree on and practice it before shutdown becomes an issue.

Similarly, coaches and students can use mounted whiteboards and white-"slates" (small hand-held whiteboards) to facilitate communication when verbal back-and-forth becomes a challenge. For instance, the agenda for the one-on-one session can be put up on a wall whiteboard before the student comes in, just as a professor outlines the class lecture up front. The slates can be used to allow time for processing or to pace the back-and-forth of the conversation.

One day when a student came in, I could tell he was really stuck. I asked him if he wanted to meet then or to wait until later in the day. When that did not work, I wrote the options on the slate: "meet now" or "meet later in the day." Luckily, I had no other structured appointments that day and could make the offer. It took a few minutes, but eventually the student tapped the "meet now" option and we continued through the rest of the agenda unabated.

Many people with autism have experienced a shutdown, but such an experience does not have to frustrate them (or their coaches, professors, or allies) if techniques like these are established early on in the working relationship. It also is not just the student experiencing frustration and communication blocks in a one-on-one session. Listen to this poetic take on the first semester from one coach's journal:

Laptops are driving me crazy! The students are all meeting in the lounge these days to play *Halo*. "S" has become quite well known over there; the other students all call him the "Halo Man" because he makes fantastic maps and posts them online—which is good.

Great for a student who came to campus and was terrified that he would never fit in.

The problem is that "S" isn't getting any schoolwork done. When he comes in for coaching, he is behind in all three classes. There's an issue with Internet connection at home—apparently it's not as good as here on campus, so he says he "has to" do his maps here, but home is good enough for homework. Trouble is, he doesn't go home on the bus until the library closes here, and he is back at dawn the next day. Again—this seems like a fantastic outcome—he likes being on campus. He's doing things on his own. He is flying away from the nest, and I am not sure what to do. I know it's rather melodramatic, but Yeats comes to mind:

> "Turning and turning in the widening gyre, the falcon cannot see the falconer/Things fall apart, the center cannot hold..."

How can I help him see that he is sacrificing the academic success he had first semester for the social life he has now?

In most ways, the issue in this illustration is an easy one to deal with, despite how decentering it is for the coach writing the journal entry. In the case of "S" and his coach, he and his parents and allies celebrated S's new social status, but he also dropped a class. This was *not* celebrated by his parents or allies. The student needs to draw the line between behavior and consequence, at the prompting of the allies. Sometimes this is a difficult task to do. Usually it goes well and the lesson is learned, but at other times, it can lead to anxiety and other emotional issues.

It is important for both the ally and student to grasp the idea that academic coaching is not therapy. Serious mental health issues may become apparent when a student regularly meets with a coach. Often, a student has a comorbid diagnosis along with Asperger's syndrome. These range from ADHD to anxiety or even bipolar disorder, and though there are ways to help students cope with some of the effects of these other diagnoses, it is best for the coach to know his or her abilities and boundaries when they arise. As mentioned in Chapter 2, in the case of something more out-of-bounds for the coach—like seeing the early signs of depression, for instance—a list of referrals and knowledge of the mental health safety nets on campus is key. The earlier students become familiar with the type and location of mental health resources available on campus, the easier it will be for the student and coach to react appropriately if or when it becomes necessary to access them.

Here is an example of why this is important, from the same coach's journal:

> "N" came to coaching today very depressed and wanting to talk to me about her trigger points again. I'm not at all squeamish about such things, but I felt that it had gotten beyond me. Together, we called Dr. Z over in Student Support/Counseling and set up an appointment. "N" seemed disappointed when I made the suggestion—maybe a little scared at opening up to someone besides me whom she didn't know so well, but she did it anyway once I reminded her that she met Dr. Z during Orientation Week.
>
> I am very glad Dr. Z came as a guest speaker back in August, and I feel certain that I did the right thing referring "N."

Group Work in Plenary

The third component of the program is group work. Over the years, a somewhat awkward name for it has stuck: Plenary. There are several reasons for keeping this name. First, though it is awkward, it is also unique. Many students have been to "group," and this usually connotes "group therapy," or "teen group." Neither of these fit. The plenary group is not led by a therapist; it functions instead more like a class on topics related to being autistic in a college setting. Furthermore, although the agenda structure is put in place by a coach, the topics raised in many of the plenary groups come from the students. The first semester is based on the answers students give on the Baker or other social skills checklists during Orientation Week. In the second semester, a unit entitled "Autism and Self-Awareness" incorporates lectures on the history and definition of autism and individual projects chosen by students. The focus of the plenary session is to assist students in understanding what autism is and how it affects them as a college student and young adult.

The term *plenary* stuck because it is much more powerful than "group." Technically, a plenary session is a meeting fully attended by all. As an adjective, it means full, complete, absolute, unqualified. In the plenary meeting of a legislative body or at a conference, the work of committees is often reviewed, summarized, and then given the support of the full body. The hope is that, in the plenary meeting of a model-two program, the individual students are given a chance to share their thoughts and experiences, then the whole group gives each individual support for their hard work.

To summarize, in model two, the whole system is connected by the "Nine Criteria for Success." It is held together by a year-long process that focuses first on scheduling and collaboration, and includes regular weekly check-ins. Finally, the goal of confidence and self-awareness is always in sight. Helping a student feel confident comes in the first semester, and then the emphasis turns toward future planning and autism awareness/identity. Although this all makes for a highly structured program, human beings are not generally so predictable.

LIVING CURRICULUM
FOR COLLEGE SUCCESS

Because of the developmental tasks before a first-year college student, adjusting to the higher education environment within the college setting they have chosen to attend is extremely important. Remember how disastrous Sally's first week was? In order to avoid Sally's situation, an institution of higher learning can emphasize *Phronesis*, or practical wisdom, and use a "living curriculum" as the basis for their program for students with autism. No matter how much is covered in a high school setting, most of what a student has to master to be successful in college depends on their actually being present at a college. Lessons learned in one context do not always translate easily to another.

Living curriculum is a term originally used in developing church-school material (Harris, 1989). Its focus is to reveal the context of knowledge and how it is taught within a given congregational setting. This concept is known in the literary criticism world as *sitz im leben*. As such, living curriculum applies very cogently to the communal environment of higher education. A living curriculum applied to higher education is wisdom-driven, process-oriented, and individualized. It has two goals, the first of which is to support student independence and self-advocacy, keeping developmental stages in mind. The second goal is to open academia to the intellectual diversity now knocking at its doors. When we place these two goals at the fore, they yield autism-specific supports that work.

The definition of *living curriculum*, as adapted here, has three parts. First, it is wisdom-driven. Prior to the scientific era, most knowledge was delivered and digested, not through controlled experimentation and the uncovering of "facts," but instead through the creation, memorization, modification, and sharing of stories. (For a compelling take on this from an autistic perspective, see the essay "When Language Fails" in Perner, 2012.) Furthermore, stories were told and retold (or read and reread) in a definite context, and usually for a definite, sometimes ritualistic or spiritual, purpose. Thus, much of the way in which we have built what we teach and how we teach it, is based on stories like those found in the Pentateuch (the first five books of the Bible), Greek and Chinese philosophy, Roman mythology, Egyptian and Mayan architecture, the Bhagavad Gita, and Indigenous peoples' oral traditions and cosmologies.

Perhaps the most common pieces of wisdom still found in the vernacular of Western culture are Aesop's Fables such as "The Tortoise and the Hare," and Christian parables such as "The Good Samaritan" and "The Prodigal Son." Just as children's books and "vacation Bible school" programs use these kinds of stories to present and make memorable life lessons, a living curriculum is designed to help students on the spectrum discover stories that they can hear, ingest, modify, and share. The wisdom traditions involve not only external stories handed down but also a process whereby such illustrations are taken in and become part of the "story of ourselves" upon which people create their own identities. We learn who we are based on stories told to us, as well as the stories of others with whom we associate.

Most colleges and universities also offer ways in which the members of their community define themselves. Behind the college logos shared in Chapter 4 are traditions built up around important athletic events, finals week traditions, and many, many other unique stories that help create a college student's identity. These stories are ostensibly there for anyone who is willing to commit four years and a pile of money to an institution, but not everyone has been included—race, class, and physical and intellectual differences have often kept certain students out of certain forms of higher education. Unfortunately, it is not just the excluded students who suffer from this, but the institutions as well.

For example, up 'til now, many folks with autistic cognition have not been able to "say" who they are. As a result, the wisdom in their stories has been excluded from the canon upon which we base our approach to knowledge. Just as literature and contributions from other disempowered groups became recognized and lauded in higher education during and after the Civil Rights Movement and the women's movement, so the stories of autistics and other intellectually diverse people will become part of the overall academic conversation, and that conversation does not just take place in journals and publishing houses. It takes place in the day-to-day lives of particular colleges, community colleges, and universities. It takes place in dorm rooms, student lounges, faculty offices, and classrooms. A living curriculum is specifically designed to provide a process for individual students on the spectrum to become confident about speaking who they are, discovering the wisdom enfolded in their own stories and in the stories of others with autism.

Look at three sample lesson plans included at the end of the Appendix and judge for yourself. The first one, "Check Your Scene," is designed on the theory of context blindness. "What Joe College Knows," the second lesson plan, works on the principle that you understand more about what you are doing if you teach it to someone else. The last lesson plan is a photo phone scavenger hunt meant to be used as students are just beginning to acclimate to the new college campus and environment. Do these lesson plans conform to the goals and ideas of a living curriculum? Are they wisdom-driven, process-oriented, and individualized? That is, do they allow the students to tell their own story—how they think and what they value as people, as well as people on the autism spectrum? Do they encourage independence and steps toward self-advocacy? If the lesson were taught at your college or university, would they demonstrate the intellectual diversity that the students participating in them represent? Would they yield autism-specific supports that work?

The curriculum, exercises, and charts in the Appendix are all subject to improvement. They are there so the readers can retrofit them to their own intellectual differences and to the particularities of their higher education institutions. This is just the beginning of a bigger, longer-lasting conversation about autism and higher education.

The curriculum of any college or university, including a living curriculum, is only a temporary vessel of knowledge, a reflection of truth. It is shaped by student input, reaction, and sometimes even student criticism. This work is seldom explicit; it is honed by the whetstone of practice, trial, and retrial. A curriculum that purports to be "living" will never be finished.

Each time it is practiced, and with every group of students it seeks to reach, there will have to be fine-tuning, lessons learned, and better methods created. Sometimes this happens in the office after the lecture has bombed. At other times, it happens right there in the classroom as a student discovers and shares new insights on the subject from his or her own point of view, insights that take the room—including the professor—in a completely unexpected direction. Theory and practice never stop dancing with each other, and this curriculum (like all curriculums) may not be the best or only music for their ballet.

However, the focus of this program of instruction is to open the door of intellectual diversity to a world of academia so that people with autism can step in and bring their unique abilities, personalities, and gifts to the process of changing higher education for the better. As students bring their gifts to academia, as the autistic mind is recognized and celebrated, as stories of people (especially individual persons on the spectrum) emerge, the construction of what is wisdom and how humans approach knowledge will be transformed. This is a very high calling worth pursuing.

SALLY AT THE FIREHOUSE

Remember Sally? She did not get back to college for a long time after her disastrous first week there. But several years later, one of Sally's allies found herself again with Sally. This time, they were in a firehouse. Sally had become interested in becoming a firefighter, and she was there to interview with the instructors who ran the Firefighting/Emergency Medical Services program.

Sally felt prepared. She had spent two summers working at a wilderness camp in a western state where she did pack training and elementary first-aid training. She was in great physical shape. She found a place at the camp where life made sense. There was structure and plenty of miles to wander. She wanted to get her professional certificate, specializing in forest-fire science, and return as soon as possible. Sally was interested in sharing with her interviewers that she had Asperger's syndrome because she knew that she was drawn to living by a code like the one the firefighters share. She believed that she could handle the physical demands, too. The biggest challenge that came from the interview was that she would have to learn to communicate with her fellow firefighters clearly and effectively, even if she did not like them or understand their viewpoints all the time. Lives depended on it.

Sally's ally knew that her friend's ultimate success depended, not just on Sally's skills and motivation, but also on the acceptance of the firefighting community as it existed at the community college where she would pursue her degree. Had Sally "grown" enough to succeed in college this time? Had the college changed enough in the intervening years to support Sally's chosen path to success?

QUESTIONS

1. No matter how a student and her institution set up support for autism in college, several driving questions will need to be addressed:

    a. What college readiness skills does each individual student already have?

    b. Where will each student need to stretch?

    c. How does autism affect each student individually?

    d. What kind of experience can each college offer its autistic students?

2. How can a student who has come to accept his or her autism also come to be accepted and supported by the institution of higher learning they attend?

3. Take a look again at the two models presented in this chapter: 1) Intake Interview and Follow-Up Workshop and 2) Orientation Week, Coaching, and Plenary. If you are a student, which model do you think would work best for you? If you are a professional, which model do you think would work best for your institution? Discuss the whys and wherefores.

4. Name one or two of the identity-shaping stories or traditions that are unique to your academic institution. In what ways have students with intellectual differences been excluded or included in them?

PART II

The Institution

Truth...

PHILOSOPHY AND AUTISM

In 2010, I was invited to lead a discussion at a renowned hospital that had just gotten a huge grant for autism research. My assumption was that the physicians and medical administrators there would be all about "curing autism," and my bias was that such a singular approach was inadequate to the task at hand. In other words, being a service provider and educator, I wished that they would spend a greater portion of their millions on treatment of autism, not just "test tubes and rubber gloves." I presented them the following pairs of words, which appeared and then faded (rather cleverly, I fancied) in succession during the first minute of my PowerPoint:

- Freud—Skinner
- Diagnosis—Treatment
- Whole—Parts
- Theory—Practice
- Autism Speaks—Autistic Self-Advocacy Network

- Medical Model—Cultural Model
- Cure—Accept

I then asked them to consider this question: when thinking of autism, what comes to mind with each pair of words? Although I expected a lively discussion, the group sat in stunned silence instead. Looking back over this experience, it occurs to me that part of the silence that ensued between them and the team I brought with me was that we did not have a common philosophy.

In my reflection, I remembered one dreary winter day in graduate school when I walked into the classroom a little early to find a two-panel cartoon sitting on the front table. On the first panel was a pug, his wrinkled eyes nearly closed in impending slumber. A shaky-edged thought bubble extended from the pug's head. It contained a picture of a dog treat followed by an equal sign and "doggie bone." Beneath it were written the words—"a realist pug contemplates a doggie bone."

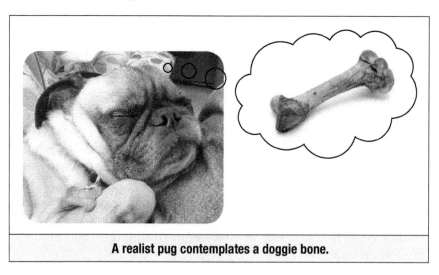

A realist pug contemplates a doggie bone.

Next to that panel was a second panel that contained the same dreamy-eyed puppy, but this time in its thought bubble was "doggie bone," followed by an equal sign and then a picture of a doggie bone. Under this panel were the words, "a nominalist pug contemplates a doggie bone."

A nominalist pug contemplates a doggie bone.

Could it be, I wondered, that this difference in viewpoint is at the heart of the most complex controversies found in the world of autism treatment and research?

Nominalism: What's in a Name?

Leo Kanner is the first person to name a small number of children diagnosed with schizophrenia whom he observed as having several common characteristics as "autistic." Afterward, many others took this label and looked for the same characteristics in hundreds of thousands of other people. "Autism" may not be merely a collection of letters we place upon a collection of real symptoms that we encounter in our society and in our schools. We may have discovered an actual human difference that existed prior to our naming it.

For those who think of autism like the nominalist pug, the name *autism* is enough to define an entire group of "others," but naming runs a dangerous course. If the truth about what autism is continues to be coalesced in only its naming, then we may be creating a kind of separate species of human being that we call the Autistic. This result is known as pseudo-speciation. Biologically, a species contains all the individuals that are capable of reproducing with one another. What generally causes the divergence of one species into two is their separation over time until genetic changes finally become so diverse that individuals from each population can no longer reproduce. Although this is, of course, not what has happened between autistics and neurotypicals, something like this happens culturally when naming becomes the primary way of defining all differences. This is compounded when the differences we name, in turn, keep people apart. From now-defunct interracial marriage laws in the United States, to South African apartheid, pseudo-speciation has long fueled the worst in humanity. We should not do this again; such alienation between autistics and neurotypicals will not lead to anything but tragedy for both.

Yet there is also an important caution to address in the concrete research upon which we define autism. In order for autism research to avoid the trap of supporting pseudo-speciation, then its participants, methods, claims, and conclusions must be carefully examined. Research and observation in the field of autism studies is often subject to the tyranny of deficit language, delusions about objective science, pop psychology, and reliance upon debunked science in a field that has grown exponentially over the past two decades, and shows no sign of slowing down. Chapter 9 returns to how the ethics of autism research are being questioned and addressed.

For now, it is clear that nominalism has its drawbacks. The name "autistic" should never become the means by which the hegemony of power that people with typically-wired nervous systems have in our institutions and our culture. What good is a name if we don't first accept the reality of that which is named in and of itself?

Realism: Was Beethoven Autistic?

So what if the realist pug is right? What if people on the spectrum did, in fact, exist prior to the 1940s when they were named? Logic and historical biography have placed many famous people on the "possibly autistic" list, including Emily Dickinson, Henry Ford, Mark Twain, Alfred Hitchcock, Bill Gates, Steve Jobs, Charles Schulz, and Beethoven. Many of us may have a less famous list of "possibles," perhaps a spinster aunt or a bachelor uncle from our own families; maybe an absent-minded professor we once studied under, or a coworker who never quite fit into the office culture.

If such people were really autistic, then what were their lives like? What can we learn from the lives they led and the way their cultures and families treated them? What made some become as "successful" as the composer of *Für Elise* or the cartoonist who invented Schroeder? What made others who never achieved the fame of Beethoven or Schulz fade from memory? Is fate as fickle with autistics as it is with neurotypicals, or might knowing even just a little about Beethoven's development have been enough to help the faculty at DCAC in Philadelphia all those years ago, find a placement that would have brought hope and joy to Anthony, the young composer?

If autism is a real condition, not just one invented and named by the dominant cognitive style, then we should not consider autistic differences to be a deficit. Instead, the variability represented by those who are on the spectrum might be seen as something that strengthens the gene pool of humanity, rather than something that we name an aberration.

The realist would say that other cultures contained people who were autistic, too; they just did not call them that name, but found them a niche in which to live and thrive. Since Kanner first named his patients "autistic," and, more recently, as brain evidence has come to the forefront, many people have come to believe that autism is more than just a name. It is, for them, a phenomenon of human diversity that is only, just now, being elucidated.

The realistic case for autism suggests that intellectual diversity is part of the human species as a whole. Intellectual differences not only mark the variability between groups of *Homo sapiens* but also drive the development of individual human beings, from childhood through adolescence and into adulthood. Without the developmental changes in brain wiring that occurs, for instance, in what some call "adaptive adolescence," people between age fifteen and twenty-five would not be as inclined to take risks, seek novelty, or associate primarily with peers. According to this view, it leaves the human race without individuals who are wired to go into novel, risky new environments and who are not driven to invest in the future world they and their peers remake. In other words, the global influence the human race has over our planet would never have happened if it weren't for the intellectual diversity spawned by the growth and development of the human brain.

The variability autism represents in the human species is evident. Variability is the organizing principle of nature. As such, it is essential for those who love and work with autistics, as well as the autistics themselves, to ponder questions related to the ethics of variability. For instance, "How can human beings delineate and adopt an ethic of variability in their daily interactions with one another?" and "How can we relate to one another in ways that will benefit us both individually and altogether?"

Cultural and cross-cultural works on autism often combine both nominal and realistic categories that lead to the contemplation of important questions on the ethics of variability. Such an ethic relies on the interdependence of individuals with autism and the cultures in which they find themselves. In the personal stories of people who love someone on the spectrum (Rupert Isaacson's (2009) *Horse Boy*) and biographical and autobiographical accounts of autistics (*Look Me in the Eye: My Life With Asperger's Syndrome*, Robison, 2007; *Aquamarine Blue 5*, Prince-Hughes, 2002; *Thinking in Pictures*, Grandin, 1995), readers encounter the poignant, often liberating, accounts of how autism affects the human condition. Works like these remind us that autism is not chiefly described as a matter of functionality or nonfunctionality (Murray, 2010), but is instead a matter of humans telling human stories. This is where teaching students on the autism spectrum begins. Where students are inspired to believe that their intellect counts and their unique view of the world that is can help to shape the world that will be. It is where professors are inspired to adapt their way of thinking about pedagogy and how they use it. Where each person's conscience may be pricked to rethink how they feel about what it means to be a person in the first place.

Exactly what autism is may not be best explained by nominalism or realism alone. Autism might better be understood as a relationship between and among human beings divided by aspects of their differences. What is of primary importance in all of our relationships and interactions with one another is the person, not the label or treatment. When we come from this human-centered viewpoint, then no Platonic pure form of "normal" stands in the way, no expectation of perfection guards the entrance to what our society means by "success," and, better still, deficit language no longer has to be our only way of defining what autism is. Instead, the neurodiversity evident in the human genome becomes a mirror for people to transform the very fabric of society, including our institutions of higher education.

TRANSFORMATION BEGINS WITH EDUCATION

Whole departments within schools are dedicated to creating and testing techniques that they feel professionals can use to provide support for those who are "disabled" according to the legal definition—but just exactly what are they up against when it comes to honoring their task as it relates to the education of autistical-ly-wired minds? Two roadblocks stand in the way. The first is how "truth" is projected and taught in the college classroom and the second is the role that context plays in the learning process of autistic students.

First, educators may be up against what Parker Palmer called the mythical but dominant model of truth (1998, p. 99). Palmer suggested that even though the word *truth* is considered a little anachronistic in today's higher education conversation, a dim echo of a time when religion-inspired voices dominated the great lecture halls of academia, an objectivist model of truth is so "deeply embedded in our collective unconscious that to ignore it is to give it power" (99). He went on to argue that there is such a thing as a "community of truth" that understands itself collectively, and each of its members individually, as gaining strength from recognizing that context matters, whether we call it something as esoteric as "the great web of being" or something as practical as the "seminar-style classroom." Palmer reminded us that there is knowledge-based teaching and people-based teaching. His approach seeks to bridge the gap—but does it succeed, especially when applied to students (or professors) with autism?

In what Palmer called the mythical approach to truth, an object is placed at the top, an "expert" at the center, and several hopeful "amateurs" below the expert and his or her ability to pass on the objective knowledge.

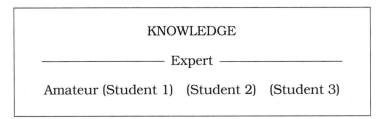

This approach is a closed system. On the other hand, in the subjectivist approach, a subject is placed at the center, surrounded by knowers. This allows knowledge, if not also truth itself, to exist in an open system. The difference between the two approaches is that a subject is available for relationship; an object is not. Furthermore, in the objective system, the expert controls the context (what little there is). In the subjective system, each knower brings his or her own context to the floor, which often leads to clashing contexts and slippery truths.

Student 1

Student 2 Student 3

Student 4 KNOWLEDGE Student 5

Student 6 Instructor

Student 7

Here is where the second roadblock for those who support students with autism shows up. Peter Vermeulen (2012) called this the theory of context blindness (Chapter 5). The definition of *context blindness* is a deficit in the ability to use context subconsciously and spontaneously to make meaning. Context sensitivity, the opposite of context blindness, is the ability to discover within the collection of elements contextually relevant information and ignore unimportant things. Context in this case includes both context inside the memories and experiences wired into the brain, and details present in the sensory input presented from the environment. Hence, context blindness does not refer to not <u>seeing</u> context but to the inability to use relevant context found in the situation to make meaning.

Peter Vermeulen makes a compelling and often fun-to-read argument that context blindness is at the heart of the differences found in people with autism. He backs this up by expanding the idea of context across several aspects of autism and general psychological research, including brain science, attention, perception, social problem-solving, facial expression recognition, speech, literal language, memory, intelligence, and social cognition. In many ways, Dr. Vermeulen's treatise is the best "unified theory" of autism we have today, for he used context to blend and add to several theories of autism including Baron-Cohen's theory of mind, the various theories of central coherence, executive functioning, and even research into neurobiological differences. At the heart of context blindness is this notion that what differentiates the brain of someone with autism from someone without autism is a lack of quick, subconscious use of context. In other words, students with autism, if context blindness is accurate, may fall behind in the typical college setting because of differences in the way they perceive what surrounds that which is being taught, and because of differences in the way they process the information. Perception and processing are two of the key elements in any pedagogy. If context blindness is correct, then that has several implications for changing and adapting how, and maybe even what, is taught in higher education.

The first implication is that it will be in the open, subjective classroom where students with autism will find it most difficult to succeed. The theory suggests autistics tend to think in one-to-one relationships, not one-to-many relationships. Therefore, in a class where the pedagogy may be to memorize lists of information in a not-necessarily-interrelated way, a student with autism may have the edge. To put it into Palmer's schema, in an objectivist classroom where truth is assumed to move from the expert to the amateur(s), the student may do quite well. However, in a subjectivist classroom, where an open, rather than closed, system of truth-telling is predominant, the student with autism may not make sense of the material.

When this idea is brought down to the level of basic diagnosis, a question comes to mind. If a person with autism has deficits in *developing, maintaining, and understanding relationships*, as the DSM-5 indicates, then will he or she be able to thrive in a classroom where relationship is key and the subject is placed at the center of the approach? If not, then how might we adapt and change our pedagogy so that students with autism perform better in college classrooms? First, might a case be made that those who support autistic students are better off guiding students toward fields where they may encounter more objective classrooms than subjective ones? If the students do find themselves in classrooms with a more subjectivist approach, then might the best accommodation be around supported self-advocacy rather than the more traditional support found in most IEPs and college accommodation forms? If students receive supports to help them relate to peers and professors, then will they do better with grades and graduation rates? Is supported self-advocacy the "magic bullet" accommodation that will work for intellectually-diverse students with autism? Perhaps the best approach is to separate out objective and subjective pedagogies so that students can be matched up to fields of study and endeavor where they may shine.

Perhaps this would work, but like all things involving humans, this approach is too deterministic. The autistic style is not just about some stereotyped and amorphous mind that can only contribute to the fields of science, technology, engineering, and math (STEM). It is more accurately about an alternative form of processing that may lead an individual into any form of endeavor. Examples of successful autistic accounting graduates abound—but so do successful autistic students called into traditionally subjective fields of endeavor like creative writing and even childcare. Furthermore, there is evidence that any person's skills and competencies may improve with age and experience, so approaching autistic differences from a strictly objectivist versus subjectivist dichotomy is too divisive and ultimately will prove too simplistic.

Still, how "truth" is understood and projected in a classroom or field of study is an essential part of getting the whole picture about the role context plays in the learning process. Also, as newly-compiled evidence points more and more to the role that context plays in the learning process of autistic students, the success or failure of these students may hinge upon how teachers and institutions form the communities of truth that exist in their college boardrooms and classrooms. All fields of academic effort exist in a community in which truth is uttered, confronted, and upheld. Palmer (1998) calls the node where "truth" and context come together the "community of truth." Further, Palmer says, in the community of truth, strength is gained by individuals and by the entire group when people recognize that context matters. Maybe our call as educators and allies is not to funnel our students into specific areas that "fit their autistic brains," but to find new ways to think about the communities of truth for whom we work. How we do this will vary depending on what part one plays in the community of truth: professor, student, or administrator.

PEOPLE WITH AUTISM, HISTORICALLY IMAGINED

Many classrooms and institutions are still based on the hierarchal understanding of what knowledge is. In fact, the idea of "university" began in the middle ages as an earthly representation of the "great chain of being,"—the creator at the top, his angels descending, and humans each in their proper place down here on Earth receiving enlightenment from the creator's hands after passing through the angels, the Pope, the Bishop, etc. In such a world, it would seem that anyone with a "difference" might be excluded, discounted, or even eliminated. However, thought experiments that my students have done lead me to another possibility:

the Middle Ages may also have been a time in history when the person with intellectual differences had a solid place in society, vital to the health of the village.

 ## "HOW I WOULD LIVE IN MEDIEVAL TIMES"

If I lived in medieval times, I would build my house a couple miles outside of the village just inside the woods. (So I didn't have to deal with people). There I would learn even more than I know already about myths, stories, and the natural world. (So I could learn more about what I love the best). I would become a healer and storyteller (since they had no video games to design yet). People would come to me for guidance and support when they wanted to know what was wrong with them or how they fit into the wider world. They would pay me or barter with me, and then I would send them back to the village.

Although this comes from the wistful mind of a student with autism, it is not at all farfetched. When Rupert Isaacson (2009) introduced his son with autism to the Mongolian people, they quickly suggested to Rupert that the lad might one day become a healer. One of the implications at the heart of Roy Richard Grinker's (2007) anthropological work on autism showed that individuals affected by autism find a place for their loved ones in their society, no matter how averse it is to the label. He told stories of Indian mothers opening public schools for children with autism, releasing them and their families from the shame and hiding that can accompany the disorder. In several cultures, including Kenyan and South Korean, Grinker found inspiring stories that began, dwelled, and ended with one concept—communities of all sorts create place and purpose for people with autistic cognition. Higher education communities of learning are beginning to do the same.

I must admit that I still secretly derive a great deal of comfort from the Platonic thought that there is a divinely-inspired pure order to the universe and that academia may resemble that order closely, as a shadow on the wall of the cosmological cave. In my best moments, however, I face the same question other educators face: "Shall we be dedicated purely to objectively advancing our field of knowledge, or shall we also dedicate ourselves to the creation of academic communities where students may discover, learn, and be inspired by the subject we love the most?"

QUESTIONS

1. Which way does your group lean—toward believing that autism is a concrete, definable condition that can be singled out in reality (the realist) or toward the belief that it is a way of grouping then naming the multiplicity of cognitive styles that human beings possess?

2. In what ways, if any, does it matter to you that there may have been others in history who were "autistic"?

3. If you have read one of the biographies or autobiographies listed in the "Realism: Was Beethoven Autistic?" section, share your response and reaction to it with others.

4. Which form of "truth" do you feel is most common in the classrooms of your institution? Does this way of truth telling vary by teacher, department, or subject?

5. Agree or disagree, and then debate sides: People with autism make better engineers and research scientists than they do helping professionals.

6. How would you live in medieval times? What aspects of your personality or cognition style does this picture reflect, if any?

7. If you are a teacher, how do you seek to inspire students with the subject you love the most? As a student, would this approach work for you?

Research

"WE MURDER TO DISSECT"

The poet Randall Jarrell, in his translation of Goethe's *Faust*, used the words, "We murder to dissect," to describe the postmodern drive to apprehend everything there is to know and reduce it to discordant bits (now bytes) of information (1976). Much of the research on autism is disconnected from the fullness and freedom of those who are autistic. On December 10, 2011, the Autistic Self-Advocacy Network (ASAN) held a symposium at Harvard University on the ethical, legal, and social implications of autism research that attempted to address this discontinuity. Flowing out of the symposium came both a critique of how autism research is funded and focused, and strong suggestions about how balance might be restored to the field of autism research.

True to ASAN's motto, "Nothing About Us Without Us," the symposium brought together an equal number of neurotypical researchers, and researchers who identified themselves as on the autism spectrum. Since 2006, the founder of the host organization for this event, Ari Ne'eman, has sat on the National Council on Disability and chaired the council's Policy and Program Evaluation Committee. In many ways ASAN and Ne'eman represent the attitude shift that began in the early 2000s, away from the disease model of autism and toward a more comprehensive set of ethics on intervention and meaningful consent that, as of this writing, is now often called the "Autism Acceptance" movement.

The first critique coming out of the symposium involved the place of politics in autism self-advocacy. By *politics*, I do not primarily mean the ideological "discussions" of this decade about "conservative" or "liberal" approaches to the size and role of government; what I mean by politics here is what Aristotle meant: it is the practical knowledge concerned with the happiness of the citizens within a regionally-defined area called a city-state (Barnes, 1984). Athens and Sparta were the chief city-states that Aristotle had in mind, and like them, the higher education institutions of today are often small, self-contained, cohesive units that contain their own rules, constitutions, enforcement mechanisms, social classes, departments, and cultural expectations. In fact, ancient city-states may arguably be seen as closer to modern learning institutions than they are to modern nation states.

As such, a description of the parallels between the modern campus and the ancient "city-state" can begin the same way Aristotle began—with a discussion of the mechanisms out of which the college is fashioned.

The mechanisms of the city-state were its "citizens" and "raw materials." For a college, this includes student, staff, and faculty. It also includes all those materials that are represented in the school budget, from classrooms to salaries to office spaces. How the citizens and the materials are intentionally mixed and utilized creates the college city-state. The "constitution" of the college delineates the ways in which decisions about this mix are made. All of those decisions ideally stem from the way that priorities are set at the college and how those priorities align with what the college calls the "good" at which it aims. This "good" is often summed up in the motto of the institution. One supposes that the motto and the current constitution and bylaws of the institution remain essentially connected at any college or university that maintains a mission in and to the world.

It is important to note here that, for Aristotle, a "constitution" is not primarily a piece of paper or a set of words. It is the very heart and soul of the city-state, and it is what makes up the heart and soul of each of its citizens. Their health and well-being, their "constitution," comes from the primary or efficient cause of the city-state's founding principles. Every aspect of a city-state, and therefore each of its citizens, aims toward this goal: "the city-state comes into being for the sake of life but exists for the sake of the good life," and the "good life" hinges upon making happiness the condition of all (Miller, 2011).

So is "happiness" the condition of all of your academic institution's citizens? What aim is at the heart of your school's motto; what purpose makes up the "good" at which your college or university aims? Do students, staff, and faculty who possess autistic cognition have a chance to experience said happiness or contribute to the common "good" set up by your founders?

Admittedly, probably fewer people involved in higher education today know their motto and the biography of their school's founder than know the name of their school's most famous or successful athlete. Furthermore, even when we put aside athletics, our best institutions will tell you that they base their approach to knowledge on research-based practices, not moldy mottos and medieval minutiae. Yet, there still may be a place for ethics like those of Aristotle to analyze modern academic practices. For though the number of journal articles, medical patents, retention, and graduation rates are now the "coin of the realm" for most colleges and universities, not every "good" needs to be bound up with "production," not every politic needs to be about the distribution of material.

The symposium sought to expand on the principle that ethics in autism research ought to include those who are autistic. It raised topics including funding research patterns since the original ADA, types of research models being incorporated, demographics in autism research, business ethics and autism, safety and self-determination, use of aversive interventions, eugenics and genetics in autism research, the diagnostics of autism, the use of deficit language, frameworks for putting values into practice, and using universal design for learning (UDL). So many ideas and responses arose that day that several books would not be enough to cover them all; however, three themes came from it: increasing the participation of people with autism in research about autism; reducing or eliminating the use of deficit language; and separating the "business of autism" from the vulnerability of consumers of autism materials.

Participation of Those with Autism in Research

The first theme, participation of autistics in research, comes out of a general criticism of how current research is conducted. The first reproach came from the effects of big money on big studies.

For instance, much of the funding for autism research coming out of ADA 1990 went first to well-established agencies that aligned with the law, but not necessarily with issues that people on the spectrum and their allies find important. Of course, these issues vary from one person to the next, but several that were raised by Scott Michael Robertson are employment, victimization, and inclusion in school and recreation. As he noted, "there is a tremendous amount of societal research on autism going on, but on what?" (Autistic Self-Advocacy Network, 2011). How can researchers be prodded to do work that is more relevant to those who are on the spectrum?

One common answer among many of the presenters at the symposium was to use research models that vary from traditional models. Sue Swenson, in her presentation, spoke of the importance of using ethnographical research designs in order to include the influence of families and cultural "norms." The other model that came up several times is called community-based participatory research, which incorporates community members as equal partners with scientists doing the research. In addition to shaping the relevance of the studies, ethnography and community-based participatory research, if used more often, would broaden the demographics to include underserved populations and people with autism who are not just children. As one presenter put it, "We have enough research now on kids and meds; it's time to see the whole population of people on the autism spectrum" (Autistic Self-Advocacy Network, 2011). Since this statement, there has been some evidence that the principal research designs that only used children as subjects, and demonstrated in their results support for theories about autism that emerged in the 1990s and 2000s, did not support those same theories when given to adult subjects with intelligence numbers within the normal range. Evidence for this, presented by Peter Vermeulen on April 4, 2014, in Olathe, Kansas, included good performance for cognitive flexibility, Theory of Mind tests, and on central coherence (Happe & Booth, 2008). Continuing to pursue broader categories of subjects, communities, and settings could help common threads be uncovered that explain a lot about what is labeled "autism."

In addition to broadening the scope and participation of those from whom data are collected, a second emergent theme at the symposium became how more autistics need to be involved in the research process. People with autism can serve on grant review boards, lead and co-lead projects, and participate in the analysis of results. As academic doors begin to open wider for people with autism, graduate and undergraduate students on the spectrum can be encouraged to enter other fields of endeavor and bring their own unique perspectives with them.

In addition, whether researchers are on or off the spectrum, whether they are conducting their fiftieth study or just publishing their doctoral work, another suggestion emerging from the symposium was to reconnect researchers with the responsibility for how their research is used. As one speaker put it, "no more *publish and forget!*"

Let's Stop That Awful Flapping: Deficit Language

A very loving and sincere person said these words in an IEP meeting for a 5-year-old child: "I think that, if we could help him control himself in class, he would do much better. Before we talk about how to help him learn to read ... can we stop that *awful* flapping?"

The second critique of research offered here stems from the ubiquitous use of deficit language, not only in IEP meetings, but also in the research that supports what interventions are proposed in them. At the 2011 ASAN symposium, the feeling was that the preponderance of published autism research shows negative results, not positive ones. If this is true, then it is important to carefully balance what studies are finally chosen for publication, not just what projects are initially funded. Other researchers at the symposium reminded the group that even the simplest sounding conclusions can be fraught with deficiency-based language and interpretations. It is as if we concluded that children on the autism spectrum laughed less at jokes—but no one ever controlled for whether the jokes were actually funny to children.

Deficit language and negative bias become more difficult when implications come from findings that further increase the cloud of negativity already looming over the definition of autism. For instance, if one were to suggest that the "laughing disability" found in this example indicates an *overall lack of empathy* in children with autism, then the science here becomes more than just problematic. It has the potential to become unethical.

Despite the insidious nature of deficit language, and how it molds much of what we believe about autism, ways to counter it are possible. First, events like this symposium can help funders, administrators, researchers, and publishers become conscious of the misuse of deficit language and make changes in the way they do their work. Second, as professionals begin to realize the role of deficit language in autism research, it becomes possible to critique, and maybe even reinterpret, studies that have been done in the past and switch to neutral language going forward. Fortunately, the scientific method has, as its main principle, the mandate to analyze, correct, and build upon its findings and assumptions; however, the effect of deficit language on individuals can be more difficult to address. Look again at the actual words that make up the DSM-5 diagnosis for autism. Here are a few of them, starting with criterion A (American Psychiatric Association):

> deficits (four times), delays, abnormal, failure, reduced, total lack of, poorly integrated, abnormalities, deficits in understanding (again), total lack of facial expression (again), difficulties adjusting, difficulties in sharing, apparent absence of interest

And these words are all present in only the first quarter of the diagnostic criteria!

The problem is not just that deficit language makes up the core of diagnostic verbiage—diagnosticians are trained to delineate aberrations, not elucidate the strengths that may exist in human diversity. No, the problem comes when a person with autism sees all these words and is asked to accept them as an accurate description of who they are. What if some of the deficit language in the DSM-5 were replaced with sufficient language? How might this change the way people with autism view themselves? What follows is an example of how we could replace some deficit language with sufficient language in working with the DSM-5 (Fig. 8.1).

FIG 8.1   Sufficient Language

Criterion	DSM-5 (Deficit) Language	Alternative (Sufficient) Language
A	**Persistent deficits** in social communication and interaction across contexts	**Deliberate strategies and unique forms** of social communication and interaction across contexts
B	Restricted, **repetitive** patterns of behavior, interests, or activities	**Focused** and keen interests and activities
C	Symptoms present in early childhood	**Different approaches to stimuli** beginning in early childhood
D	Symptoms together **limit and impair** everyday functioning	Symptoms often **challenge** the autistic person's **inclusion** in neurotypical society

To its credit, the new DSM-5 autism diagnosis is not completely rigid. It incorporates a continuum of severity in its description of autism's effects from "requiring support" to "requiring very substantial support" in an attempt to conceptualize the "spectrum" concept first introduced by Uta Frith (American Psychiatric Association, 2013). This helpful tool seeks to emphasize the effects of autism on everyday functioning rather than pigeonhole all autistics into the same category of need. Despite this, the best impulse of caregivers and allies, and the best attempts for autistic people to accept their disability, are often overshadowed by the diagnostic dependence on what cannot be done instead of by the acknowledgement of who a person is in their totality. In this way, the "disease" is dissected, but the "patient" is murdered in the process.

What if we tried to write the IEP mentioned earlier in a different way? What if instead of insisting that flapping be medicated away, the concerned IEP team member in the opening illustration of this section were given the support he or she needed to accept the flapping? Then concern might give way to curiosity. What is it about the flapping that helps the child? Is there a way to harness the energy burn and comfort that comes from the flapping and put it into another activity, or maybe just help the child put boundaries (when, where, how long) on the flapping that keeps it part of the routine but helps it not interfere with other things that are equally important? Perhaps flapping does not have to be set out on the table at the IEP—or even in the classroom—with the word "awful" placed in front of it. How might just removing the derogatory language change everyone's approach to the child's needs? Furthermore, what if this same approach was taken to the practices of a young adult college student like the one here, for whom flapping is no longer an issue, but who has accepted the need for physical release, focus, and comfort through movement, and even exposed others to its benefits:

> I used to flap a lot. I loved to look at what it did to my hands. I realized that I could not flap in public during grade school without being made fun of. Then a wonderful teacher in fifth grade taught me that I did need to do something physical when I was stressed. She taught me to walk the hall before class when things get too complicated for me. She accepted the need I had for physical release. Her acceptance turned into understanding myself better. And then last year, something hilarious happened. One night when we were bored, I taught my roommate to flap, and she loved it. Now the

whole dorm floor flaps for fun. When finals week comes along, we even have flapping contests. It's great!

Change the language, and you change the meaning. It seems obvious, but it is not always so. Two memorable phrases came out of the discussion about deficit language at the symposium. The first: "Sometimes I think that the only thing that unites people who are on the spectrum is how they affect the rest of us. Neurotypicals come up with names and descriptors to make sure that 'they' remain 'them' so that we never have to really think about 'me' or 'us.'" The second phrase speaks directly to the main thrust of the "communication deficits" in DSM-5 299.0:

> I'm on the spectrum, and I played telephone as a kid. I know all communication involves both listening and talking. So, research that supports the idea that "deficits in social emotional reciprocity," "deficits in nonverbal communicative behaviors," and "deficits in developing and maintaining relationships" are only a problem for people like me seems skewed from the start.

Vendor Mania: Autism as Business

The third critique that emerged from the symposium involves the use of research for business purposes. This critique seeks to separate the "business of autism" from the vulnerability of consumers of autism materials. At the risk of "biting the foot that stomps my own grapes," autism has become a huge business, and like all flourishing businesses, much good, but some bad, has come of its meteoric growth.

Go to any autism conference and you will find hundreds of people whose livelihood is connected to autism. Medical, educational, and administrative professionals often cover the floor of the exhibit hall with booths full of treatment systems, packaged curriculums, adaptive gadgets, and the latest CDs, DVDs, and even (gulp!) books on autism. Like any flooded market, the business of autism poses several practical, ethical, and existential questions.

First of all, how are all the new businesses approaching the phenomenon of autism? What is their reason for existing? Like the realist and nominalist pugs from earlier in the book, some exhibitors are banking on a Platonic view of autism—the belief is that there is a *pure form* of "autism" that can be apprehended, usually by reason and the use of scientific method. This "autism" does not on-balance affect humanity in positive ways, so the negative effects of it are addressed by treatments (or cures) that can be marketed and sold. For a business with this approach, the goal is to assist everyone in recovering from autism so that autistics can more closely correspond to the neurotypical, or ideal pure form, of humanity.

On the other hand, pragmatic businesses exist who do their work simply because they think that it will be useful for people with autism. They do not pay special attention to the "big problem of autism," but instead are concerned with the day-to-day efficacy of that which they promote and produce. Pragmatic enterprises seek to alleviate, not eliminate, the problems and challenges that sometimes arise from autistic cognition, or even just to provide a public outlet for those affected by autism—a place where they can "tell their story" and feel safe.

Neither approach is inherently wrong. Although having no autistic cognition left in the gene pool is the extreme form of the cure approach, most business men and women are not this extreme. Their goal is to reduce the amount and severity of negative effects from autistic cognition. Although pragmatists may not have as solid a scientific basis for their products and techniques, their strength is that they place the autistic person at the center of their business plan. The problem with either approach comes when any business willingly or accidentally victimizes the people who come looking for support and hope. How does this happen? One of the main reasons this can occur is because of something psychologists call cognitive dissonance in decision bias. Briefly put, the more expensive a choice is, the stronger the belief becomes that it is the right choice.

Leon Festinger first developed the notion of *cognitive dissonance* in 1957. It quickly gained popularity in public discourse. Many aspects of business, marketing, and even theology are now influenced by this concept (Komarnitsky, 2014). For parents, allies, and even unwary professionals who are out to spend resources on autism materials, cognitive dissonance can influence thoughtful decision-making. As they spend more and more money on particular curricula, go more frequently to workshops on particular ideas, and pore over books and articles on specific claims for cause and cure, the reputations of the businesses that promote these items increases. Many important breakthroughs in science and culture come through the open marketplace; however, the ethical business making money in the autism marketplace needs to be aware of the influence of cognitive dissonance in its customers' decisions and be careful not to believe its own press too readily.

An open marketplace for autism products needs to have checks and balances. First, the consumer must be wise and wary. For this to be the case, open conversations have to replace "camps" when it comes to what works for autistic people. Second, the human propensity to oversimplify must be set aside. Causes and cures for autism—from mercury to wheat germ—have appeared in the popular press, and these and others like them will continue to garner curiosity and support. However, serious questioning, solid research, and thoughtful and respectful argument have to be maintained in order for passionate belief to give way to real and effective understandings of autism.

Finally, people with autism must be included in the conversation! The most important consumer of autism business is the autistic person him- or herself. Those of us who are allies have a job to do in the autism business: to focus on educating the consumer with autism on how to sort out when their own autistic differences become disabilities that may need intervention. We can trust them, and guide them if they are too young, to make decisions about what resources really work for them, and how, and how much they spend in the world of vendor mania.

STUDENTS CO-CREATE THE SERVICES THEIR CAMPUS PROVIDES

Students, remember that you are more than the research suggests. Along with faculty and staff, you are the co-creators of the services the campus provides. Knowledge is power: if you are a person on the spectrum, know your diagnosis and its effect on you. That will help you negotiate the research-based undercurrents being discussed about autism in public and in your personal, private, or professional life. It will help you be the authority on the part of the phrase *a person on the spectrum* that really matters—namely you, the *person.*

If you are a person who guides or teaches young adults with autism, then help them choose people who are autistic (famous and not-so-famous people) to look up to as they decide where they stand on the important issues of the day regarding autism.

To all "citizens" of each academic "city-state": seek out people with autism on your campus and in your hometown. Become involved in seminars, workshops, author talks, and training experiences offered by your state and local advocacy organizations. Speak up, but do not shout down. Find a dozen ways that you and your fellow autistics contribute positively to your campus environment and make them known to faculty, staff, fellow students, and especially administration. Find a dozen ways in which you think the campus could improve its acceptance of autism and the services it provides to support those on the autism spectrum, and find those who can make them known to the campus population.

Go be the best you can be and take autism along with you in your "toolbox" of gifts and graces.

 CHOOSING SIDES

Upon presenting the argument for approaching autism as a diversity issue, not disease, to a mother and grandmother of two autistic children, she brought up this heartfelt concern:

> I understand how equality and diversity are lauded in an autistic child like my son. He has Asperger's syndrome, and except for being considered rather "odd" most of his life, he has always done better when he was coached how to stand on his own two feet. What I have trouble with is my grandson. He has been severely autistic his whole life, and even now still lives in a group home with constant care. I would not want one of the boys' futures or happiness to be sacrificed for some "approach." My grandson needs psychoactive medicines, or better yet, a cure; my son needs a manners class. They are both autistic.

 QUESTIONS

1. What type(s) of research have you read about autism? Have you seen exclusion bias or deficit language in what you have read?

2. Have you ever been to a conference or large gathering on autism? Describe what you experienced there and what you were feeling.

3. What role has someone's acceptance of who you are or how you behave played in your life?

4. What advice or words of understanding would you offer the grandmother in the final story?

Transformation

Building a Community
of Interest

M oment of truth time: The average college classroom contains an overabundance of ego. This isn't a bad thing, usually. Some of the best professors are quite full of themselves—at
least when it comes to their subject matter. Most of their successful students are also quite certain that they know more than
the professor, at least on one subject or another. The whole thing
works pretty well until the professor discovers that this is, in
fact, the case.

Many students come to college with exceptional knowledge in
one area or another. I once had a student who knew all the "mil-
lennial math problems," for instance, and solving one of them was
his lifetime goal. Many students have done a great deal of reading
or remembering in some other topic, say the Civil War. Usually,
when a student discovers that they know something the professor
does not, they either keep it to themselves or have the communication skills necessary to share it appropriately with the teacher.
Not always.

THE LECTURE ON ROBERT E. LEE, OR "HOW THE PROFESSOR FELL OFF HER HORSE"

A survey history course is an ungainly, even ridiculous, thing. History of religion departments often cover all of Hebrew history in one semester, for instance, and all of Christian history in another. Even American history cannot be crunched into ten or fifteen weeks easily. Most teachers know this, so they have an era or two that they concentrate on because it is their specialty.

All was going well in one survey course until it came to the Civil War. The student with autism who sat in on the course had stayed relatively quiet until that day. The professor had not complained about the student's occasional commandeering of the lecture, and the student had never told the professor that he had Asperger's syndrome. Then she wandered into the student's area of expertise.

"Robert E. Lee rode his favorite horse, Wanderer, all the way through the Civil War," the professor said in the middle of her lecture on a Wednesday afternoon.

"That was not Lee's horse's name," the student blurted out. The professor insisted. An argument ensued. Students were released early for fear of a new civil war breaking out.

Fortunately, the student and the teacher both had the sense to resolve the issue immediately after class. So instead of ending up in a Behavioral Intervention Team meeting in the dean's office, the Internet prevailed, and the teacher learned that the actual name of Lee's horse was not "Wanderer" but "Traveller" (yes, with two Ls). It took a little more time and intervention by the disability services advocate, but the freshman student also learned that no matter how important it is to set the teacher straight, this task is best left until after class—not in the middle of it.

TRANSFORMING INTO A COMMUNITY OF INTEREST IN AUTISM

Transforming a higher education community ultimately depends on many individuals, including older students, professors, staff members, and administrators. When all these people come together to address the effects of autism, not only in a classroom but also on an entire college, they form an autism interest group. If given enough time and attention, such a group can truly change the entire community in which they live and learn.

Community is defined here as a group living in the same area and having a sense of common ownership and interests. A higher education institution has aspects of each of these characteristics; it is a community regardless of what kind of school it is. For instance, at four-year residential colleges, students actually come together to live (at least temporarily), but even two-year and commuter colleges share in the sense of belonging and common ownership that marks a community. All people who attend the same college find themselves at least partially defined by the interests or specialties of the campus. Some schools may be known for their agriculture program, perhaps others for nursing. All schools are collections of sub-interest groups, too. Besides the obvious athletic team, fans, and boosters, a school may also have fantastic dramatic arts groups or active anime clubs. So whether residential or commuter, colleges are communities with common cultures and a sense of mutual ownership and interests.

Still, it is important to recognize that a four-year stay in a dorm with all the associated drama or trauma need not be "college" for all students. For people with autism residential challenges often outweigh academic ones. In response to this, many four-year schools have begun to provide single-person accommodations or special residence halls and personnel for their autistic students. This is an important key step and is not the only approach for a student on the autism spectrum who is pursuing a degree.

Another approach is to encourage students to attend a nonresidential program first so that they may get used to the demands and changes to routine that academics requires. After a year or two, the student can transfer and start attending to issues related to living in a dorm if they like, or they can find their own living arrangement that is conducive to their needs. Eating or sleeping in a stressful sensory situation is not for everyone, and that is OK. A variety of pathways to earning a degree—and a variety of degrees to earn—are now available, so it is easier for well-coached students to make decisions about their future academic careers that incorporate their individual autism-related concerns. No one community is right for all students with autism. A student on the autism spectrum can now carefully consider and choose an experience that suits his or her needs.

This freedom of choice, however, does not let schools off the hook. It is not enough to say, "We cannot accommodate intellectual differences here, but we encourage those with them to find another place." Recent court hearings have tested the legality of supporting intellectual differences, but more than just a legal precedent is at stake. The challenge for higher education communities remains now, as it has been since the ADA began, to provide access to education for all types of people, including those with hidden disabilities like autism.

A community that is open to those with intellectual differences will require all its members to be aware of what intellectual differences really are and be committed to supporting the success of those who have them. What does such a community look like? If you excuse the semantic intrusion, answering this question hinges on the words "of interest in autism."

As stated earlier, a community is at least partially defined as a group of people with similar interests. A higher education community that truly has an "interest" in autism and intellectual differences is committed to processing and tracking the *objective* nature of autism—the numeric scope of affected people, the emerging genetic and brain science related to the spectrum, and the best practices for teaching and learning alongside those with ASD. This community is also aware of the *subjective* nature of the phenomenon—it is not just numbers, brain scans, genetic markers, and didactic practices and theories, but actual people with names, both incoming students and longtime professors who have or are affected by autism. This is what makes autism "interesting," literally between (inter-) the objective and the subjective state of being (-est). A higher education community that can maintain the inherent tension in this *interesting* state is the one that will attract the most autistic students and reap the benefits of having them be an active part of their campus milieu.

The word "of" in the phrase "community of interest in autism" also provides some clues as to what the community looks like. The genitive in any given language (the "of") is an inflection pattern that expresses origin or ownership. Just as the hammer in "the hammer of Thor" ultimately belongs to him, so the higher education community "of interest in autism" has come to recognize that the people in its ranks who are autistic belong there. The community that recognizes that it is "of autistic people" (as well as all other kinds of people) forges a stronger understanding, acceptance, and commitment to support intellectual differences as a result.

"Of" is not just genitive; it is also descriptive. The hammer that Thor wields is imbued with the Norse god's power and personality. Therefore, it is that the school that works hard to include people with autism can sometimes become known as the "college where autism is accepted." Its reputation becomes linked to its approach to intellectual differences. It is difficult to know about Colorado State University, for instance, without knowing who Temple Grandin is; closer to my home, Marshall University is as linked to its decades-old autism program as it is to its storied football team. As the scope and number of students on the spectrum continue to increase, there will be even more postsecondary schools and programs that are at least partially described as "a great place to go if you have or are interested in autism."

STARTING A STUDENT-LED ORGANIZATION

In order to create or maintain a community of interest in autism, it is vital to foster and encourage *student-led organizations*. Two aspects of this are important to cover. First, you don't have to reinvent the wheel; several organizations are out there that can help in this endeavor. One of the best comes out of ASAN, a Washington, DC-based organization whose mission is to foster leadership on campuses across the country. Second, include both autistic and neurotypical students and staff in the process. Many student-led organizations fail because the passion to have a voice on campus far exceeds the presence of the available skill sets to organize the necessary meetings and events. This is true of many differently-themed student organizations, but in the case of autism, one of the common challenge areas is executive functioning skills and time management. In order for a student-led organization to succeed, it has to have someone who can make calendars, organize events, and effectively remind participants to come to those events. This is the best way to represent the presence and influence of intellectual differences on a campus. This does not mean that an all-autistic student-led organization on a campus is doomed, but it may mean that people desiring to start one have to look extra hard to find leaders with the right skill set to make the group a success.

Checklist for Starting a Student-Led Organization "of Interest in Autism"

❑ Find out the guidelines for student-led organizations at your college. Rules vary, but usually include requirements like obtaining a faculty sponsor and naming several officers. This information usually comes from a department with a name like "Student Support" or "Student Life." Frequently a dean's office is associated with this part of a college.

❑ Create a strategic plan for your first three meetings prior to having your first meeting.

❑ Gather at least six to ten people who are interested. It is best if more students participate than faculty or staff, but at least one or two faculty or staff are usually required to "sponsor" an organization.

❑ Get each of them to invite one to three other people to the opening meeting.

❑ Make sure that at least one of the founding members really likes taking notes (or minutes), and ask that person to be the secretary, at least initially.

❑ Ask one person (can be faculty or student with experience) to lead the first meeting.

❑ Make the first meeting upbeat and open.

❑ If someone knows how to lead a brainstorming exercise or other creative idea-gathering activity, get them to do it. If not, try a website like http://thenextweb.com/lifehacks/2012/06/04/how-to-moderate-a-brainstorming-session/

❑ Keep an accurate list of the ideas, hopes, and concerns generated during this session.

❑ Before the first session ends, and while everyone is still there, schedule the next meeting.

❑ FOLLOW UP with each person face-to-face or by phone. Do not rely on email alone to help attendees remember what happened and what comes next.

❑ Get information out to the community as soon as possible on what this organization is, why they would want to join it, and when and how they can become involved.

TEACHING TEACHERS "ACCEPTANCE"

An adage of anthropology is that culture begins when specialization occurs. Every campus culture has specialized professionals whose job is to teach a specific subject; administrate a particular aspect of campus life like recruiting, finance, or registration;

or provide services like food, grounds-keeping, or public safety. Such narrow foci become a problem when "silos" develop—and the academy is frequently full of such isolated and insulated towers. The goal of doing a training on the effects of autism is to make it part of the common knowledge that everyone shares, not just the public safety officers or the psychology department.

Common knowledge about autism is very important because not every student with autism is going to self-disclose to every college worker, nor should they have to. In order to be prepared for this, faculty and staff training may begin by identifying seemingly bizarre unlabeled behaviors in a class or campus setting. These may include:

- unusual eye contact,
- being argumentative,
- having a rich vocabulary but poor use of language and difficulty producing written work,
- having a tendency to make comments that are deemed irrelevant or that interrupt,
- problems stemming from personal space or social distance,
- knowing more than the instructor in certain areas (like the name of Robert E. Lee's horse) and sharing this too freely, and
- difficulty coping socially and emotionally in group projects.

These are a few of the signs that a student may have difficulty on campus. The presence of behaviors like these is not what derails student success; instead, what causes it all to go off track is the assumptions that are made when such behaviors are observed.

For instance, during one autism and higher education in-service workshop, both faculty and staff were working with situations in which a student seemed argumentative. The professionals were then asked to complete the phrase, "The student was…" Here were some of their responses:

- "On drugs;"
- "Not properly prepared for college by their K–12 experience;"
- "Dodging because they did not do their reading;"
- "Depressed or manic;"

- "Just obnoxious;"
- "Letting their hormones do the talking."

Discussion afterward revealed that when the faculty or staff person's response is based solely on their initial reaction, the whole situation could spiral out of control and even end in a disciplinary action for no good reason.

More than one autism support program has started because someone noticed that too many students with autism were appearing in college disciplinary hearings or in the files of their public safety department. The presenting violations of a student code of conduct range from the trivial to the tragic. Examples include prosecutions for disrespect to sexual harassment. On the other side, students have also been unjustly flunked or brought to tears by ill-informed teachers or classmates who reacted instead of understanding. Slowing down the process and accepting the possible autistic origins of behavior are crucial to avoiding unnecessary outcomes.

Now, most college teachers and staff who have been in the business for any length of time know that their kneejerk responses to students are not always accurate, and they usually have learned how to back off and reassess what is going on. However, even the wisest among them may discover that a student that they really like to work with, but who has autism, still seems unable to understand and meet their academic expectations. Whether it is challenging behavior or below-average academic performance that the student is presenting, what many untrained professors may not know is that autism may be the most accurate explanation for what they are seeing (see Fig. 10.1).

If a student is autistic, the perceived behavior may come from a variety of effects of the condition. It is difficult to begin this part of the training process without reducing it to a series of generalized deficit statements. For example, "The autistic student has no sense of humor and is unable to get the professor's sarcasm," or "The autistic student always has narrow and intense special interests that block her from seeing the big picture the professor is trying to get across." Yet, it is essential for trainees, both faculty and staff, to understand that certain conditions related to the effects of autism may not be absolute, but are definitely pertinent. Furthermore, these conditions do not have to be understood as deficits anymore if the community comes to realize that the behaviors in question come, not from drugs or malicious intent, but from one of the effects of autism.

FIG 10.1 Moving From Assumption to Acceptance

See This/Think That	Realize It's Autism (the Effects of the Autistic Condition)	Do This Instead
Poor eye contact/On drugs; did not do reading	Social challenges Sensory differences	Agree on an "I'm listening indicator"
Argumentativeness/ Rebellion; hormones	Special interests Literal/Concrete thinking Superior intellect	Use a parking lot
Rich vocabulary; poor use of language/Talking back	Literal/Concrete thinking Language construction	5-Minute meetings
Difficulty producing written work or notes/Lazy; unmotivated	Sensory differences	Movement breaks Frontload the notes
Tendency to make irrelevant comments or interrupt/ disrespectful	Social challenges Executive function deficits Special interests	30-Second think
Problems with personal space and social distance/ Rude, perverse	Social challenges	Model social space and how to ask for space (with autism students and neurotypicals)
You are encouraged to discuss and fill in these last two sections of the chart yourself: What might you do as an instructor to deal with a student who knows more than you do (as in the illustration about General Lee's horse)? As a student, what might you do to help someone be more successful with group work?		
Knows more than the instructor on their "special interests"/ Showing off, know-it-all	Superior intellect Special interests	
May have difficulty coping socially and emotionally in group projects/Antisocial	Executive function deficits Social challenges	
Note: Table is also available in the Appendix.		

Columns B and C are further explained as follows:

Moving From Assumption to Acceptance: Effects of the Autistic Condition (Column B)

- *Executive Function Deficits*—impulsivity, organization, time management
- *Literal/Concrete Thinking*—affects humor and general comprehension
- *Language Construction*—intonation, modulation, and syntax
- *Sensory Differences*—both hyper- and hyposensitivity
- *Social Challenges*—does not easily recognize another's point of view or the "hidden curriculum" in a social situation
- *Exemplary Intellect*—memory that is more accurate than peers or professor in a narrow area
- *Special Interests*—perceived as narrow and intense

Moving From Assumption to Acceptance: What Techniques May Be Helpful, (Column C)

- *Agree on an "I'm listening indicator"*—This is a nonverbal way for the student and instructor to communicate that the student is paying attention. It can be the student's hand on a desktop or any other gesture that both agree on in lieu of eye contact or other neurotypical ways of showing interest.
- *Use a Parking Lot*—A "parking lot" is a section of the board where ideas or information brought up in class, but not immediately relevant to the lecture, may be written or "parked." This allows the instructor to complete the scope of his or her lecture and also validates the student's input or question. The class may return to the parking lot at the end of the lecture or on a later day.
- *5-Minute Meetings*—The student and instructor may agree to have regular 5-minute meetings before or after class or at alternative times in order to delve more deeply into a subject, clarify the notes, or otherwise review or reinterpret the information together.
- *Movement Breaks*—Many students, not just autistic ones, require physical releases or movement breaks from time to time. These can be as elaborate as leaving for a self-timed

interval and returning or as simple and subtle as squeezing one's hands together under the desk—whatever works, as long as both the instructor and student agree it is not a distraction for the rest of the students.

- *Frontload the Notes*—Because many students are visual learners, it is helpful if they can receive notes ahead of the lecture time. It is important again that instructors approve of this. Regular accommodations may also include volunteer note takers and the use of recording devices.

- *30-Second Think*—The 30-second think is a way of allowing all students to have adequate time to process a question. With this technique, the class is told that they are to each think of a response to a question that is coming up, and that they will all be given 30 seconds to do this. No one is to say anything before the time is called; then each student is encouraged to share their response. The use of a visual timer helps this work even better.

- *Model Social Space and How to Ask for Space (with autism students and neurotypicals)*—Many techniques exist on how to model social space for little ones; however, college-age people face new challenges regarding social space that they may have not had before. Ask both men and women to share what feels comfortable to them and what feels "sketchy" or even downright "creepy" when it comes to physical space. This will vary with the nature of the relationship between the people, but bringing it out into the open may help alleviate discomfort and social faux pas; it may even prevent issues pertaining to harassment. Note that at the minimum, students should be asked if they mind being touched by others. A light hand on the shoulder or arm may be OK for one but extremely threatening to another.

Although many theoretical constructs seek to explain the effects of autism, it is important to recognize that the effects of autism in higher education, like any other complex phenomenon, are not easily reduced to a linear process. Such a format can lend itself to deep and practical discussions among faculty and staff that can ultimately make a difference to everyone's approach and attitudes. Couple this approach with real examples, or better yet, include real students with autism, and real change can occur.

WRITING ABOUT A SCULPTURE:
THE FRONT/BACK DISASTER

On the second day of an autism training session that used the "Moving from Assumption to Acceptance" table, an English teacher brought forth a student paper that she wanted to discuss. The assignment had been to go to the nearby museum of art, select a piece to write on, and follow a writing prompt that said, "In your essay, explore the artwork's subject, color, medium, and its meaning. 4–5 pages."

She brought in an essay written by a student on the spectrum. She did not give the student writer a passing grade for several reasons. First, the paper was simply too short and incomplete. Next, her comments to the student noted that the paper did not provide enough sentences to help the reader visualize the artwork. Finally, the professor tagged the fact that the student turned in the assignment printed on the front and back of the page when the syllabus "explicitly stated that only one-sided assignments would be accepted."

Unfortunately, at least part of her reason for bringing the paper to the session seemed to be that she wanted to justify her belief that "students with Asperger's syndrome should not be let out of mastering the basic writing requirements of the school as taught in English 101." Before the discussion began, a more experienced professor in the same department gently pointed out that "letting students out of English requirements" was not even on the table, nor was it the reason for requiring the training session on supporting autism that they were currently attending.

Nevertheless, the initial conversation supported the English teacher's frustrations. Indeed, many professors from several departments noted that they too had returned papers for similar reasons, and not always to students with autism, either. For many, the "why" normally focused on the usual suspects—inadequate preparation, too many distractions, and some even questioned the campus curricular emphasis on process writing. They all agreed that they knew what they were seeing.

As the facilitator had them go through the "Moving from Assumption to Acceptance" chart, some possible effects of autism on this student's composition emerged. The faculty members were led to new explanations in this case. This in turn led them to wonder how things could be done differently, not to "excuse" a student from requirements, but enhance the chance that the student would be able to accomplish the assignment successfully. Below is a summary of some of the questions and ideas that the professors shared.

Executive functioning issues lead many freshmen to inadequate preparation. This student may have lost the original assignment and directions. (Was it on the web?) How does the student think? (Does the lead-up to the assignment provide any coaching for students to go from describing the artwork to elucidating its meaning)? After a lengthy discussion of the effects of autism, the small group decided to rewrite the assignment, bearing in mind other factors like supporting the sensory preferences of students and explicitly asking the students to link the requirements to their own interests and knowledge. They even wondered aloud what the best approach would be to help a student with autism negotiate the social challenges of going off campus to an unknown space like the art museum and interacting with unknown people like those at the museum's admissions desk. Perhaps the most important result of the discussion was that the instructors truly realized that adjusting assignments to meet the needs of those with differences improves the overall curriculum and helps all students accomplish more and understand the requirements of the assignment better.

The epilogue goes this way. The inexperienced teacher seemed unmoved during the discussion, but a few weeks later, the teacher approached the facilitator at an unrelated event. With a smile, she reported that the student had been frequenting the writing lab and that she, herself, had been mistaken about the "one-sided only" turn-in rule. After class the week before, she and the student had looked at the online syllabus and, sure enough, the student's memory was on target but the teacher's memory was not. Not only was the rule not on the syllabus, but the syllabus actually encouraged two-sided turn-ins to save resources. The teacher went on, "I have learned so much through this that I'm going over to the department now to volunteer to be on the Freshman Composition course revision committee." Note: sometimes the best way to teach composition to college students is to adapt and modify K–12 texts. See *I Hate to Write* (Boucher & Oehler, 2013). It has several useful tips for student writers who are on the autism spectrum.

When individual teachers learn to accept intellectual differences and understand them, departments often follow suit. When departments come to accept the effects of autism on some of their students, all of their students benefit. Sometimes accepting teachers find that they may again experience the joy of the masterpieces they were introducing their students to in the first place.

REBELLION VS. DIFFERENT WAYS OF BEING

What looks like rebellion may be merely a different way of being. Carl Jung, the great thinker and early psychoanalyst, believed that everything that irritates a person about others could lead them to a better understanding of themselves (Jung, 1958). It is unwise and even insulting to suggest that every misunderstanding generated between a student and professor is the result of the effects of his or her autism. Sometimes, people just do not get along. Their interests or opinions collide. Their personalities clash. Yet many people believe that we only grow as people or academic institutions when conflict occurs. Several current and popular Internet sites continue to channel Jung with this quote: "[Our] vision will only become clear when we can look inside our own heart. Who looks outside dreams; who looks inside, awakes."

People encounter their dreams when they look outside in the everyday interactions they have with their fellow human beings, but people awaken when they take those experiences and look inside to figure out how to process them. That is how individuals grow, and a modified version of it is how institutions grow as well. Communities are dynamic organisms. They move from tried-and-true to attempted-and-tested, and then back again. Their members alternatively dream and awaken, as Jung would remind us to do. The effects of autism on college campuses is helping us all do just that, dream and awaken to new possibilities both grand and ordinary.

Nothing is more important for the health and vitality of the higher education enterprise than incorporating human beings with intellectual differences like autism. The final reason to build a community of interest in autism is so that we can encourage the flow of shimmering dreams and new discoveries. This is the *raison d'être* of higher education; it is the way humanity finds new ideas about old truths.

RIBBON TREES AND OLD-SCHOOL PROFESSORS

When it comes to the section on how and why to start a student-led organization related to autism, I often show a slide. The photograph depicts an event suggested by a colleague from the psychology department. The idea was to invite the entire campus community—faculty, staff, and students—to hang a brightly-colored ribbon on a particular tree as they pass by if they have autism or if they have been affected by someone who does.

In the photograph, three people gather around a short tree on campus that stands beside the walk to the bookstore. As the audience takes in the slide, I ask them to tell me which person (or persons) is autistic, and which is neurotypical. I also ask which person describes him- or herself as an "old-school professor," which person is on the staff, and which is a student. Occasionally, someone will attempt to answer the questions, usually because they actually know those in the photo. However, the point is never lost. Autism, and any intellectual difference, is an invisible disability. Yet the community that lives with its effects every day need not be. Forming any sort of organization, or designing and directing a faculty training, is hard work—sometimes doomed to garnering no general interest, let alone influence, over the policies and debates that encircle the larger campus community. But those of us reading this book know how important it is to do this anyway.

As the semester crept from the glory of mid-autumn to the drear of early winter, the beautiful leaves of the tree all dried up and fell to the ground. The flashing bright reds, oranges, yellows, blues, and whites of the autism ribbons filled the limbs with color. That was what everyone saw. We can only hope that the vision continues to have an effect on what they do.

QUESTIONS

1. What assumptions about how the class will run are made on the first day of class by professors and by students?

2. Is there room in the grading system of your college for wondering "why" a students respond the way they do in class or on a test or in a term paper?

3. What are the "something(s)" your campus or college is "known for"?

4. What are some of the advantages and challenges to creating an autistic student-led organization on your campus?

5. How can your campus be more inclusive in the way it accounts for the effects of autism on its daily mission?

6. Pick two or three "issues" you might see in a classroom and run them through the "Moving From Assumption to Acceptance" exercise on pages 110–111, To what degree is this process helpful or useful?

7. Which character in the "Front/Back Disaster" has the most responsibility for achieving a positive outcome on the assignment, the student or the professor? Why?

8. Are the effects of autism on your college campus helping your community "dream and awaken" according to Jung's quote? How?

9. Allow the people in your group who have an invisible disability like autism lead a discussion on what it is like to live with it on a daily basis. Perhaps begin by sharing the list of things they do on a typical day at college.

Twirl and Spin

I n 1985 when I was working at the Philadelphia school system's DCAC, the term *autism* was confined to the brains of only a few psychiatrists and a small batch of parents and loved ones, but my whole career began to twirl and spin that spring in ways that I am only now, thirty years later, beginning to understand. People whose brains light up differently than my own, and whose hearts have been too long underappreciated and misunderstood, have always been present. Each time I encounter a person on the spectrum, whether it is one of the 18-year-old college students I work with, or my 10-year-old grandson, I feel like an X-ray is taken of my own soul. For me, when those days in Philadelphia come to mind, I realize in a flash just how diverse the themes and variations are that make up the world.

In the second creation story presented in Genesis, God brought all the beasts of the field and the birds of the air to the freshly created *adamh,* or earth being, to "see what the man would name them; and whatever the man called each living creature, that was its name" (Genesis 2:19b, NIV). Indeed, humans seem to have always used our power to name the world. It is our nature to search for and find the common threads among the multiplicity of phenomena—bird and beast, event and impression—that everywhere confronts our senses, and reduce all that rococo to a set of labels and monikers.

This reductionism gained the status of a driving force in the mid-18th century at the height of the enlightenment, when Carl Linnaeus, the person who created our current system of natural classification, wrote in the preface to his 1735 *Systema Naturae*: "the creation of the Earth is the glory of God, as man sees only the works of nature." He believed that the study of nature would reveal the divine order of God's creation, and that such naming of nature would reveal this divine order in the universe to human beings.

Our understanding of nature and science is far from that which Linnaeus had, and yet, the great movements in science have all followed this noble principle in the three hundred years since. With each subsequent classification system—from biological evolution to the "quarks" of particle physics, to the diagnosis of modern psychiatry—scientists seek to find and name the natural phenomena they discover and thereby bring order to the world.

Several people I have known who are on the spectrum would resonate with Linnaeus, Darwin, Murray Gell-Mann, and George Zweig (the latter two independently named "quarks," the tiniest particles of protons and electrons, in 1963)—and indeed, with the whole practice of naming and classifying the world. To look at the autistic's tendency to have an encyclopedic knowledge of terms and conditions about one or more particular topics is to understand that much of science and scientific vocabulary builds upon this very skill. Stephen Shore, in *Beyond the Wall: Personal Experiences With Autism and Asperger Syndrome* (2003) and in his standard presentation about his own life as a person on the spectrum, lists scores of what he calls "special interests." If the human tendency is to name things, then the tendency of certain humans on the spectrum is to excel in the naming of certain things.

The irony that arises is that the same human propensity to designate pieces of experience to a category has also contributed to the marginalization of people who are not neurotypically wired. In fact, the whole "discovery" of autism began when Leo Kanner set about to find a common label for eleven children who had been diagnosed with "childhood schizophrenia." As he came to know the children and their case studies, he found that they had several characteristics in common. Kanner wrote that in all eleven children, "There is from the start an extreme *autistic* aloneness that, whenever possible, disregards, ignores, and shuts out anything that comes to the child from the outside," (Kanner, 1943, 242).

So it is that Kanner employed the term *autism* for the first time as a diagnostic category separate from the term "childhood schizophrenia" to distinguish kinds of behaviors that would come to be associated with the "fascinating peculiarities" of the children he studied in 1943. The term *autism*, from "auto" or "unto itself," became so successful that it is still used today. How people perceive autism has changed drastically—especially in the past twenty-five to thirty years. In recent decades, the prevalence of the autism diagnosis has increased. Although some still refer to this as the "autism epidemic," most people have come to realize that autism is better thought of instead as a culturally significant phenomenon that is now being understood and responded to in new and creative ways. Even institutions that have received grants to do medical research on autism now tend to join in with Roy Richard Grinker's assessment of the phenomenon. He said that it is time to get away from seeing the increase in autism as a frightening public health tragedy, and instead said:

> But what if, paradoxically, the rise in rates of autism as gathered by schools, epidemiologists, and public-health officials is evidence not of tragedy, but of good? (What if) ... the newer, higher, more accurate statistics on autism are a sign that we are finally seeing and appreciating a kind of human difference that we once turned away from and that many other cultures still hide away in homes or institutions or denigrate as bizarre? The results of the new rates are that we are fortunately seeing more research, more philanthropy, and more understanding of how families struggle to cope. (Grinker, 2007, 5)

Students, teachers, professors, school counselors, and college advisors can begin to be part of this new wave to the extent that they approach autism as a "culturally significant phenomenon" in ways that do not reduce students with autism to trending curves on a statistical chart. All human beings, as well as the communities in which they live and work, are in a constant state of transformation and development. Now is the time for higher education to be transformed by what is being learned and shared by those on the autism spectrum in our classrooms and on our faculty, and the opportunity to be transformed does not come solely from those who are in the field today. The wisdom has been there a long time, and it comes from the mouth of babes just as assuredly as it does from the writings of learned professors and gifted researchers.

LIGHTNING BUG, BUT NOT IN A BOTTLE

My mind sometimes goes back to a 7-year-old girl who, in 1985, on a walk through Fairmont Park, Philadelphia, informed me in a flat voice that "scientists have named about 1,000,000 different kinds of animals; 800,000 of them are insects."

She went on as a lightning bug gently explored the back of her little hand. "Insects have six legs and three body parts: the head, abdomen, and the thorax." She never looked up as she recited a few more facts to me in her monotone voice. After that, she started to whisper a phrase: "don't put me in a bottle, don't put me in a bottle, don't put me in a bottle," and she kept that up for 5 minutes. Then my young mentor went silent. The firefly flew away.

I wonder where she is today. What is she doing? Has she gone on to write a dissertation on her discovery of the 800,001st insect? Has the world had a chance to become lovelier, more fascinating, and more complete because of that little girl and the remarkable flash of her autistic mind?

QUESTIONS

1. Do you or others in your group resonate with the scientists mentioned in this chapter and the systems they created?

2. To what degree do you agree or disagree with the idea that categorization contributes to the marginalization of people who are autistic? Under what conditions might categorization help science grow?

3. Some have suggested that Leo Kanner, the one who coined the term "autism," may have been autistic himself. Share what you know about Kanner and discuss this suggestion and whether it is relevant to modern dialogue about autism.

4. Discuss this definition of acceptance: "The per-
    sonal, cultural, and political act of acknowledging
    and receiving persons with autism as people who
    possess another form of human diversity."

5. How is your institution being transformed by
    the effects of autism and those on the spectrum
    coming and working at it? If you can, cite specific
    trends, attitude changes, programs, and evidence
    you see that autism is being "accepted."

References

American Psychiatric Association (2013). *Diagnostic and statistical manual of mental disorders* (5th ed.). Arlington, VA: Author.

American Psychiatric Association (1994). *Diagnostic and statistical manual of mental disorders* (4th ed.). Washington, DC: Author.

Americans with Disabilities Act Amendments Act of 2008 (ADAAA), 42 U.S.C. 12101 et seq.

Americans with Disabilities Act of 1990, Pub. L. No. 101-336, 104 Stat. 328 (1990).

'Ask first at Antioch.' [Editorial]. (1993, October 11). *The New York Times*. Retrieved from http://www.nytimes.com/1993/10/11/opinion/ask-first-at-antioch.html

Aspy, R., & Grossman, B. G. (2007). *The Ziggurat model*. Shawnee Mission, KS: AAPC.

Attwood, T. (2006). *The complete guide to Asperger's syndrome*. Philadelphia, PA: Jessica Kingsley Publishers.

Autistic Self-Advocacy Network (2011, December). *Symposium on ethics, legal and social implications of autism research*. Cambridge, MA: Harvard University.

Baker, D. L. (2006, January). Neurodiversity, neurological disability and the public sector: Notes on the autism spectrum. *Disability and Society, 21*(1), pp 15–29.

Baker, J. (2005). *Preparing for life: The complete guide for transitioning to adulthood for those with autism and Asperger's syndrome*. Arlington, TX: Future Horizons.

Barnes, J. (Ed.; 1984). *The complete works of Aristotle*. Princeton, NJ: Princeton University.

Baron-Cohen, S. (1997). *Mindblindness: An essay on autism and theory of mind*. Cambridge, MA: The MIT Press.

Bettelheim, B. (1972). *The empty fortress: Infantile autism and the birth of the self*. New York, NY: Free Press.

Boucher, C., & Oehler, K. (2013). *I hate to write.* Shawnee Mission, KS: AAPC.

Chapman, G. D. (1992). *The 5 love languages.* Chicago, IL: Northfield.

Chickering, A. W., & Reisser, L. (1993). *Education and identity* (2nd ed.). San Francisco, CA: Jossey-Bass.

Driscoll, R. D. (1972). Parental interference and romantic love: The Romeo and Juliet effect. *Journal of Personality and Social Psychology, 24,* 1–10.

Ellis, D. (2012). *Becoming a master student* (13th ed.). Boston, MA: Wadsworth Cengage Learning.

Emerson, R. W. (1847). Self-reliance. In Emerson, *Essays, First Series.*

Erikson, E. H. (1980). *Identity and the life cycle.* London: W.W. Norton and Co., Ltd.

Erikson, E., & Erikson, J. M. (1997). *The life cycle completed.* London: W.W. Norton & Co.

Family Educational Rights and Privacy Act (20 U.S.C. § 1232g; 34 CFR Part 99), 1974.

Festinger, L. (1957). *A theory of cognitive dissonance.* Stanford, CA: Stanford University Press.

Festinger, L. (1962). Cognitive dissonance. *Scientific American, 207*(4), 93–107.

Filler, C. (2010, March). *Statistical update on students with autism.* Columbus, OH: Ohio Association for Career and Technical Education, Special Needs Division.

Gioia, G. A., Isquith, P. K., Guy, S. C., & Kenworthy, L. (2000). *Behavior rating inventory of executive function.* Odessa, FL: Psychological Assessment Resources.

Goethe, J. W. (1976). *Goethe's Faust, part I: An English translation.* (R. Jarrell, Trans.) New York, NY: Farrar, Straus and Giroux.

Grandin, T. (1995). *Thinking in pictures.* New York: Vintage Books.

Grandin, T., & Barron, S. (2005). *Unwritten rules of social relationships.* Arlington, TX: Future Horizons.

Grinker, R. R. (2007). *Unstrange minds: Remapping the world of autism.* New York, NY: Basic Books.

Gross, Z. (2013). Better living through prosthetic brain parts. *Navigating college: A handbook on self-advocacy written for autistic students from autistic adults.* Washington, DC: Autistic Self-Advocacy Network. Retrieved from http://www.navigatingcollege.org/ download.php

Happe, F., & Booth, R. D. (2008). The power of the positive: Revisiting weak coherence in autism spectrum disorders. *Quarterly Journal of Experimental Psychology, 61,* 50–63.

Harris, M. (1989). *Fashion me a people*. Louisville, KY: Westminster/John Knox Press.

Isaacson, R. (2009). *The horse boy: A father's quest to heal his son*. New York, NY: Little, Brown & Co.

Jung, C. G. (1958). *The undiscovered self*. New York, NY: New American Library.

Kanner, L. (1943) Autistic disturbances of affective contact. *Nervous Child, 2*, 217–250.

Koegel, L. K., & LaZebnik, C. (2009). *Growing up on the spectrum*. New York, NY: Penguin.

Komarnitsky, K. (2014). Cognitive dissonance and the resurrection of Jesus. *The Fourth R, 27*(5).

Little, M. C. (2012, July 19). *NRF releases 2012 back-to-school, back-to-college consumer spending reports*. Retrieved from https://nrf.com/news/retail-companies/nrf-releases-2012-back-school-back-college-consumer-spending-reports

Linnaeus, C. (1735/2013). *Systema naturae* (in Latin). Charleston, SC: Nabu Press.

Liptak, J. J. (2011). *College survival and success scale* (2nd ed.). St. Paul, MN: JIST.

Maslow, A.H. (1962). *Towards a psychology of being*. Princeton, NJ: D. Van Nostrand.

Mayerson, A. (1992). *The history of the Americans with Disabilities Act: A movement perspective*. Retrieved from http://dredf.org/publications/ada_history.shtml

Miller, F. (2011). Aristotle's political theory. *Stanford Dictionary of Philosophy*. Retrieved from plato.stanford.edu/entries/aristotle-politics/

Murray, S. (2010). Autism functions/The functions of autism. *Disability Studies Quarterly 30*(1).

Myles, B. S., Trautman, M. L., & Schelvan, R. L. (2004). *The hidden curriculum: Practical solutions for understanding unstated rules in social situations*. Shawnee Mission, KS: AAPC.

Ne'eman, A. (2013). [Foreword.] *Navigating college: A handbook on self advocacy written for autistic students from autistic adults*. Washington, DC: Autistic Self-Advocacy Network. Retrieved from http://navigatingcollege.org/download.php

No Child Left Behind Act of 2001, Pub.L. 107–110, 115 Stat. 1425.

Palmer, P. (1998). *The courage to teach*. San Francisco, CA: Jossey-Bass.

Perner, L. (2012). *Scholars with autism: Achieving dreams*. Sedona, AZ: Auricle Books.

Prince-Hughes, D. (Ed.) (2002). *Aquamarine blue 5: Personal stories of college students with autism.* Athens, OH: Swallow Press/Ohio University Press.

Reynolds, C. R., & Kamphaus, R. W. (2004). *BASC-2: Behavior assessment system for children* (manual, 2nd ed.). Circle Pines, MN: American Guidance Service.

Robison, J. E. (2007). *Look me in the eye: My life with Asperger's syndrome.* New York, NY: Crown.

Roux, A. S. (2015). *National autism indicators report: Transition into young adulthood.* Philadelphia, PA: A.J. Drexel Autism Institute, Drexel University, Life Course Outcomes Research Program.

Shore, S. M. (2003). *Beyond the wall: Personal experiences with autism and Asperger syndrome* (2nd ed.). Shawnee Mission, KS: AAPC.

Shore, S. M. (Ed.). (2004). *Ask and tell.* Shawnee Mission, KS: AAPC.

Sicile-Kira, C. (2006). *Adolescents on the autism spectrum: A parent's guide.* New York, NY: Perigee.

Silberman, S. (2015). *Neurotribes: The legacy of autism and the future of neurodiversity.* New York, NY: Avery.

Stanfield, J. (n.d.). *The circles curriculum.* Retrieved from http://www.stanfield.com/ products/family life-relationships/social-skills-circles-curriculum-intimacy-relationships

Tolstoy, L. (1886/2009). The death of Ivan Ilyich. *The death of Ivan Ilyich and other stories.* (R. Pevear & L. Volokhonsky, Trans.) New York, NY: Alfred A. Knopf.

Vermeulen, P. (2012). *Autism as context blindness.* Shawnee Mission, KS: AAPC.

Vermeulen lecture, Olathe, KS, April 4, 2014

Vygotsky, L. S. (1978). *Mind in society: The development of higher psychological processes.* Cambridge, MA: Harvard University Press.

Williams, S. (2005). *Reflections of self.* Grandville, MI: The Gray Center.

Wilson, M. A., & McClane, M. (2012). Ohio autism in higher education survey. Unpublished manuscript.

Wolf, L. E., Brown, J. T., & Bork, R. (2009). *Students with Asperger syndrome.* Shawnee Mission, KS: AAPC.

SUGGESTED READING LIST

For Practical Information

Bedrossian, L. E., & Pennamon, R. E. (2007). *College students with Asperger syndrome: Practical strategies for academic and social success.* Horsham, PA: LRP Publications.

Harpur, J., Lawlor, M., & Fitzgerald, M. (2002). *Succeeding in college with Asperger syndrome.* Philadelphia, PA: Jessica Kingsley.

Myles, B. S. & Adreon, D. (2001). *Asperger syndrome and adolescence.* Shawnee Mission, KS: AAPC.

Myles B. S., Cook K. T., Miller N. E., Rinner L., & Robbins, L. A. (2014). *Sensory issues and high-functioning autism and related disorders* (2nd ed.). Shawnee Mission, KS: AAPC.

Ne'eman, A. (2013). *Navigating college: A handbook on self-advocacy written for autistic students from autistic adults.* Washington, DC: Autistic Self-Advocacy Network. Retrieved from http://navigatingcollege.org/download.php

Wolf, L. E., Brown, J. T., & Bork, R. (2009). *Students with Asperger syndrome.* Shawnee Mission, KS: AAPC.

For Inspiration and Motivation

Carder, S. (1995). *A committed mercy.* Grand Rapids, MI: Baker Books.

Emerson, R. W. (1847). Self-reliance. In Emerson, *Essays, First Series.*

Frankl, V. E. (1969). *The will to meaning.* New York, NY: Penguin.

Grinker, R. R. (2007). *Unstrange minds: Remapping the world of autism.* New York, NY: Basic Books.

Isaacson, R. (2009). *The horse boy: A father's quest to heal his son.* New York, NY: Little, Brown & Co.

Jung, C. G. (1958). *The undiscovered self.* New York, NY: New American Library.

Maslow, A.H. (1962). *Towards a psychology of being.* Princeton, NJ: D. Van Nostrand.

Palmer, P. (1998). *The courage to teach.* San Francisco, CA: Jossey-Bass.

Peck, M. S. (1978). *The road less traveled.* New York, NY: Simon and Schuster.

Perner, L. (2012). *Scholars with autism: Achieving dreams.* Sedona, AZ: Auricle Books.

Prizant, B., & Fields-Meyer, T. (2015). *Uniquely human: A different way of seeing autism.* New York, NY: Simon & Schuster.

Shore, S. M. (2003). *Beyond the wall: Personal experiences with autism and Asperger syndrome* (2nd ed.). Shawnee Mission, KS: AAPC.

Williams, S. (2005). *Reflections of self.* Grandville, MI: The Gray Center.

Appendix

List of Resources in Appendix

FOUNDATIONS OF AUTISM AND ACADEMIC SUCCESS

Preparation: Key to a successful debut as a college student is getting the student and her or his allies involved in the preparation plan the summer before and, most of all, putting the student in charge of the plan as the first day approaches.

Developmental stages: An 18-year-old on the spectrum is still an 18-year-old; therefore, when allies coach toward competence, fidelity, and love, students understand and accept who they are and that there are others who want to help them grow.

Competence: Time is the student's only commodity; make time for time (management). Teaching students how to master their own time in their own way is the ally's most important task.

Identity: Allies: respect adult students; students: claim your identity, be realistic about your strengths and your academic challenges, *and seek support.*

Intimacy: A program or an ally can provide tools to unmask the "hidden curriculum," but in the end, the student has to step out, and seek out, friends and dates on his or her own terms and learn to cooperate with his or her instructors.

Accommodations: Students on the spectrum may receive accommodations that do not contribute to their academic success.

Two models: Students achieve success in higher education by learning their own data at intake to determine how ASD will affect them academically and then allowing that information to shape the way they approach their certificate or degree program.

Truth...: Effective support of intellectual differences is based on seeking truth with practical wisdom that promotes independence and quality outcomes.

Research: Students are more than what the research suggests.

Transformation: Transforming the academy and changing the academic success rate of students with autism requires awareness within an entire higher education community committed to supporting intellectual differences.

PREPARING FOR COLLEGE

Autism View Rating

(Same rating sheet done by student, parent, teacher, other)

Section 1				
Student Name				
Email or Phone				
Date				

Section 2				
Please rate how often you do the skill by marking one box to the right. Please put one mark in each row. Do not skip any rows.				

	Always	Usually	Sometimes	Seldom	Almost Never
Social Skills					
Waits turn to speak					
Participates in small groups successfully					
Respects others' opinions					
Sensory Issues					
Stays in one place throughout structured time					
Stays focused and is not distracted					
Manages own sensory needs appropriately					
Time Management (Context)					
Is prompt to class or appointments					
Meets deadlines					
Creates and follows schedules					

	Always	Usually	Sometimes	Seldom	Almost Never
Self-Advocacy					
Express myself with confidence					
Seeks assistance when unsure or confused					
States opinions and relays needs clearly					
Thinking Style					
Handles constructive criticism well					
Know how I learn best					
Thinks concretely/literally					
Organization					
Files papers and assignments routinely					
Finds items quickly when needed or asked					
Breaks large tasks into small, workable parts					
Flexibility					
Sets obtainable goals					
Independently makes short-term decisions					
Adapts to a change of routine effectively					

COMPETENCE
Kinds of Time/Prioritizing

Dead Time: Short periods between classes with nothing scheduled

Free Time: Longer periods that *should* be scheduled (free time isn't really "free")

1. Break
2. Fitness center
3. Lunch
4. Gaming time
5. Clubs
6. Hanging out in student center
7. Read for fun

Study Time: Scheduled 1-hour blocks for keeping up with classes. Should fit two-to-one formula)

1. READING for class
2. TEST/QUIZ preparation
   a. Memorizing
   b. Going over notes
   c. Assignments
3. WRITING
   a. Ideas
   b. Outlines
   c. Drafts
   d. Editing
   e. Final
4. RESEARCH
5. GETTING SUPPORT
   a. Instructor
   b. Meeting with coach (2–5 hours)
   c. Writing lab—library
   d. Computer lab
   e. Tutoring center
   f. Disability services
   g. Advising/Counseling
   h. Science, Technology, Engineering and Math (STEM) education
   i. Autism Club meeting

My College Schedule for: (Week)

	Monday	Tuesday	Wednesday	Thursday	Friday	SA/SU
8:00						
9:00						
10:00						
11:00						
12:00						
1:00						
2:00						
3:00						
NOTE						

Student's Week Schedule Block
Numbered Study Planning

Student takes 8 hours of coursework. She needs to study an additional 16–24 hours to succeed (2:1 or 3:1). She can do this by filling in the 24 hours of the day on her schedule. She could trade off a few daytime hours for weekend or evening hours if she has appointments, friends, activities at school, and so on.

	Mon 25	Tues 26	Wed 27	Thurs 28	Fri 1	Sat/Sun 2-3
8:00	1	2	3	4	5	
9:00	6	7	8	9	HUM 1001 9–12	
10:00	1:1 with advisor	10	11	12		
11:00	12.5	13	13.5	14.5		
	Transition Time	Transition Time	Transition Time			
12:00	15.5	16.5	Plenary Group	17	Exercise at Gym	
				Transition Time	Transition Time	
1:00	ENG 1100	18	ENG 1100	Check-In	ENG 1100	
2:00	19	JAPN 1101 2-4	20	JAPN 1101	21	
3:00	22		23		24	
Evening	Transition Time	Transition Time	Transition Time	Transition Time	Transition Time	

Example Student Assignment Record

ENG 251 (%)

Assign	Date	%	Grade
Essay 1	4–26	25%	25/25
Essay 2	5–12	25%	25/25
Essay 3		25%	20/25
Quizzes		25%	

HUM 111 (points)

Assign	Date	Pts	Grade
Lec 1	4/2	5	5
Lec 2	4/9	5	5
Lec 3	4/16	5	5
Art Paper	4/21	50	42
Lec	4/30	5	5
Midterm	5/5	100	91
Lec	5/7	5	5
Art Paper	5/19	50	49
Lec 8	5/21	5	5
Lec 9	5/28	5	
Lec 10	6/4	5	
Pop 1	4/4	10	9
Pop Q2	5/10	10	8
Participation (10 pts/day)		200	170

IDENTITY

The "How Will I Know If I'm Ready for College?" Exercise

Instructions:

1. **Instructor**: Fold C behind B, then fold B and C behind A; give to students.

2. **Students**: Begin by making a list of what you are good at under Column A. Try to be specific and include only one item in each row.

3. **Students**: Now make a list of what you expect to be good at in college under Column B. Try to imagine yourself in college as you make this list. Keep the items as specific as you can.

4. **Together**: Look at Columns A and B and see what matches and what "misses." Tally how many matches the entire class has, and how many misses. Discuss any common matches or misses.

5. Now unfold Worksheet 1 and carefully read through the list under Column C. This list comes from the experiences of actual first year college students.

6. On Worksheet 2, compare Columns B and C first. Make a separate list of the matches and the misses between your list and Column C.

   a. Think about these questions:

      i. Were there more matches or misses?

      ii. What match is most significant to you?

      iii. What miss most surprises you?

   b. Were your expectations regarding the skills needed for college realistic?

7. Finally, compare Columns A and C. Again, make a list of the matches and misses between what you are good at and what you are expected to be good at in college.

   a. Think about these questions:

      i. Were there more matches or misses?

      ii. What does the number of misses say about your readiness for college?

      iii. Which match did you expect? Which miss did you not expect?

   b. How can our program help you gain the real skills you need for college that this exercise highlights?

Worksheet 1: (Fold C behind B, then fold B and C behind A; give to students.)

A	B	C
What I'm Good At	**What I Expect to Be Good At in College**	**What I'm Expected to Be Good At in College**
		Finding classrooms, faculty, facilities, and departments
		Knowing what each department and faculty person does
		Talking to advisors about the classes I want and why
		Talking to instructors about issues that come up in class
		Talking to other students about classes and working in groups
		Talking to other students in order to make friends
		Organizing college assignments, due dates, and homework
		Managing my time to get homework done consistently
		Knowing when I need some help with academics
		Knowing where and from whom to get academic help on campus

A	B	C
What I'm Good At	**What I Expect to Be Good At in College**	**What I'm Expected to Be Good At in College**
		Knowing what my learning style is and telling instructors
		Knowing what my study preferences and style are
		Knowing where to go for food and fun on campus
		Knowing the course catalog and programs of study criteria
		Knowing what I need to do to get into a program of study
		How to pay for classes; when to get financial aid
		How, when, where, and what books to get
		Different class types— hybrid, web, traditional
		Knowing how to schedule classes and scheduling problems
		What to do with different teaching styles (lecture, lab)

Worksheet 2: Comparing Column B and C

Matches	Misses

Worksheet 3: Comparing Column A and C

Matches	Misses

Marbles and Diversity, Marbles and Disability

1. Look at four marbles and sketch each one on the chart under Column 1.

2. Listen and look while the techniques for categorizing marbles are explained. Then fill in the name of the category you think each marble falls into in Column 2.

3. Brainstorm different marble games and other reasons to collect marbles. Write the ideas on the back of the lab sheet.

4. Come up with ideas on what you can "do" with this marble—games, displays, sell, and so on. Put some of those ideas in Column 3.

5. Now think about the value of each marble—how much you would pay for it. Put a value on each of the four marbles in Column 4.

6. Here are some statements about marbles. Get in line, and after each statement is read, step forward as many steps as you agree with the statement. Step backward as many steps as you disagree with the statement. We will have a discussion each time.

    a. Each marble is a "little piece of art."

    b. No two marbles are exactly alike.

    c. Identifying marbles by their characteristics is interesting to me.

    d. I have enjoyed playing games with marbles in the past.

    e. Broken or beat-up "out of round" marbles are useless, even if they are colorful.

    f. I would be willing to spend up to $100 on a marble if it were really cool.

7. Here are some statements about people. Get in line, and after each statement is read, step forward as many steps as you agree with the statement. Step backward as many steps as you disagree with the statement. We will have a discussion each time.

    a. Each person is a "little piece of art."

    b. No two people are exactly alike.

    c. Identifying people by their characteristics is interesting to me.

    d. I enjoy being with many different kinds of people.

    e. Broken or beat-up people are useless, even if they are colorful.

8. Complete the four sentences at the bottom of the lab sheet.

9. When you think of how autism affects/describes you, what part is diversity, and what part is disability?

Lab Sheet: Marble Diversity

Sketch Marble (#1)	Category? (#2)	Ideas (#3)	Value it (#4)

INTIMACY

Circles

1. Go over the results of the Social Skills Menu (Baker, year).

2. Describe Circle Idea. Have students stand and get in circle with each other playing parts. One student is the "self" and the other students play "friends," "classmates," etc.

3. Questions

    a. Can a person move from an inside circle to one farther out?

    b. *Name two to five ways that you have moved a person from an outside circle to an inside one.*

        1. _____

        2. _____

        3. _____

        4. _____

        5. _____

4. Activities

    a. On a worksheet—or on your own paper—put as many people's names in each circle as you can.

        i. Now, in a different color—draw a line inward or outward for anyone you would like to move from one circle or another—for ex. a classmate that you would like to befriend

        ii. Get with another person and describe how you might accomplish this; then they will do the same with you: *Write a brief summary here of what you and your partner discussed:*

           _____

           _____

           _____

           _____

           _____

           _____

b. Take one of the above examples and act the move out

    i. Fishbowl it (comments from the outside)

        1. How do students in a college setting do this (vs. K–12)?

_____

_____

_____

_____

_____

_____

        2. Have you ever done this yourself? Did it succeed?

_____

_____

_____

_____

_____

_____

Example:

Your Circle:

ACCOMMODATIONS

Student–Instructor Interaction Checklist

To be used when writing a script and for instructor feedback after the first meeting.

Student's Name: _____

Instructor's Name: _____

Date: _____

❑ Student set up appointment according to Instructor's hours of availability

❑ Student arrived on time

❑ Student entered appropriately

❑ Student identified themselves as on the autism spectrum

❑ Student shared that he/she learns differently than neurotypical

❑ Student explained one area for improvement

❑ Student stated their goal(s) related to this area for improvement

❑ Student asked for instructor's support

❑ Student offered specific suggestions about how to get support

❑ Student negotiated with instructor on the specific kinds of support and how to achieve the goals

❑ Student asked instructor to return (this form) within 1 week either by interoffice mail, email, or before/after class

❑ Student thanked instructor for his/her time

❑ Student exited appropriately

Comments:

Example Script 1

I have Asperger's, which includes ADHD in the diagnosis. These two factors attribute to my inability to stay focused on certain things for extended periods, leading me to move around or become distracted by outside influences easily. It is my goal to reduce these incidents in two ways, the first being to fiddle around with a pen or pencil or two and to tap my foot as silently as possible. This will hopefully allow me to pay more attention in class. Today I am asking you to allow me to do this. I would like to return in 2 weeks both to hear suggestions that you feel would better solve this issue as well as feedback.

When you are finished with the form I have handed you I would appreciate it if you would return this form by interoffice mail or by handing it to me before or after class.

Thank you for your time.

Example Script 2

I have Asperger's syndrome. This makes me learn things differently than most other people. One way it affects me is that I have a hard time understanding the hierarchy of notes and knowing which ones are most important. My goal for this quarter is to understand which notes to study so I can get a high "B" on the exams this quarter.

I would like your assistance in this problem. Could you make a section more noteworthy when you're talking about important parts in your lecture? It doesn't have to be too much, just something as simple as saying "This is important" will suffice.

Could you please return this form to me within a week either by email or by handing it to me before or after class?

Activity Checklist With Comments–Short Form

My Name: _____

Activity, Group, or Event: _____

Date or Time: _____

Comments: What did I do, who did I meet, what did I like, what do I wonder about, what will I do next as a result of this. (Use additional paper if necessary)

_____

_____

Activity Checklist With Comments

My Name: _____

Activity, Group, or Event: _____

Date or Time: _____

Comments: What did I do, who did I meet, what did I like, what do I wonder about, what will I do next as a result of this. (Use additional paper if necessary)

What did I do?	
Who did I meet? (name)	
What did I like (or dislike)?	
What do I wonder about?	
What will I do next as a result?	

Example Advisor Appointment Feedback Form

My Name: _____

Person Meeting With: _____

Date and Time: _____

Short Summary—What I asked, What I learned, What I do next

Asked:

Learned:

What I do next:

Highly-Charged Language

Highly-Charged Phrase: *I Feel Like I'm Going to Hit Someone*

Example in Context	Why a Student Might Use It	What It Means in Context	What Can Happen as a Result	Alternative
Lab—Too much noise	Hypersensitive to sound	Code of Conduct E4a (p. 51) Threatening: implying or causing physical harm...	Professor HAS to take action: separate student, call Public Safety	Keep it to yourself or say "It is too noisy in here; I need to step out."
At lunch in the student union—too much noise	Hypersensitive to sound	"This place is noisy! I can't eat lunch here."	Friends leave with you or you go alone	Say, "Let's go to a quieter place for lunch" instead of the highly charged phrase.

"Highly-Charged Language" (Based on E4 of the Code of Conduct, XYZ University)

If you use the words: "threaten," "intimidate," "harass," "haze," or "stalking" from the Code of Conduct, be sure that you understand the highly charged nature of the word in different contexts. Follow-up and legal interdiction is REQUIRED once certain words or phrases come out of your mouth. So, use them wisely.

Look at the chart below and weigh the situations, then come up with an alternative.

"Highly Charged" Phrase	Context(s) (Change the contexts)	Why a Student Might Use It	What It Means in Code of Conduct	What Can Happen as a Result	Alternative
I really think that you should loan me your calculator for the weekend. (said 20 times)	Fellow student keeps saying this over and over	Don't have money for their own calculator	E4b (p.51) *Intimidation—* pressuring another unreasonably	Charges can be filed by receiving student; loss of friendship; calculator gone	
Don't let her sit here with us in the lounge; She totally has ASS-bergers.	Joke among friends in the gaming clan	Trying to make friends, be funny	E4c (p. 51) *Discriminatory Harassment—* speech or conduct depriving access, enjoyment, benefits to campus	Loss of friendship; hurt feelings; isolation; charges filed	
If you want to hang out with us, you have to drink this concoction—all of us did it.	Club rule or group pressure when you come to your first club meeting	Trying to prove him- or herself to others	E4d (p. 51) *Hazing—* endangering behavior as a condition for affiliation	Physical illness; unnecessary pain or humiliation; charges filed	
Saying: "This guy is stalking me" to a faculty member or a Public Safety officer walking by.	Student's behavior is annoying you, and he or she won't let up after being asked to	Feels annoyed or wants to get his or her friend in trouble	E4e (p. 51) *Stalking—* repetitive menacing pursuit interfering with peace and safety	Campus employee MUST report this to authorities	

College Confidence Survey

(Given Pre- and Post-Orientation)

Name: _____

Date _____

Please circle ONE number that matches your confidence level for each statement below.
1 NOT confident; 2 Somewhat confident; 3 Confident; 4 Very confident; 5 Sure

1. I know how to get my accommodations met at XYZ University.

        1   2   3   4   5

2. I understand and can follow the Student Code of Conduct.

        1   2   3   4   5

3. I am comfortable meeting with one of my college instructors 1:1 to discuss class work and/or my accommodations.

        1   2   3   4   5

4. I am confident that I will be able to achieve passing grades at XYZ University.

        1   2   3   4   5

5. I have a clear plan for my future that will help me reach my goals.

        1   2   3   4   5

6. I am comfortable participating in XYZ University–sponsored activities and clubs.

        1   2   3   4   5

7. I know how to schedule my classes each semester.

        1   2   3   4   5

8. I feel confident that I can find the key buildings, classrooms and offices on the XYZ University campus and independently transport myself to/from campus

        1   2   3   4   5

9. I feel confident about my knowledge of autism and how it affects me as a person and as a college student.

        1   2   3   4   5

10. *On the back, please comment on your own experiences being a student with autism? What are some of the challenges, rewards, and/or complications?*

Two Models of Campus-Wide Resources

Student's Criteria for Success: Student Responsibility and Allied Supports

Category	#	Student Criteria for Success	Student's Responsibility	Program's Consultative Supports
INDEPENDENCE	1	Access Office of Disability Services *Appointment Checklist*	Make and keep appointment and follow through	Assist in paperwork, introductions/ implementation of services; monitor ongoing academic challenges
	2	Independently schedule classes *Independent Registration*	Utilize advising services effectively; learn how to use website to get information; register and choose courses and major	Provide coaching and connections on registration, advising, and classes with fading support
	3	Independently transport self to/from campus and around campus locations *Year-end Attendance*	Follow instructions and/or lessons on accessing buildings and transportation	Provide transition services regarding transportation options
SOCIAL COMPETENCY	4	Negotiate peer and student–instructor relationships *Student–Instructor and Appointment Checklist*	Attend modules, make and keep appointments with instructors	Teach social skills modules; academic mediation; raise faculty awareness and provide faculty instruction on autism
	5	Participate in at least two nonacademic activities or events *Checklist with Comments*	Attend and write-up at least two nonacademic activities or events	Provide connections and information on campus events and clubs; encourage attendance and involvement

	6	Understand/follow Code of Conduct ***Completion of Instruction*** ***No Disciplinary Actions***	Attend, learn, and pass module on the Code of Conduct (85% or better)	Teach module on Code of Conduct; monitor behavior issues if they arise; mediate with Public Safety if needed
FUTURE PLANNING	7	Identify goals and develop a plan to reach them ***Student Future Plan***	Attend modules and transition meetings; interact with Campus Transition Resources	Provide transition coaching on employment, life planning skills, future plans
	8	Choose a program of study; achieve passing grades ***GPA 2.0 or better on Transcript***	Organize study plan and follow it; attend all classes; self-advocate; use writing and math labs; do your best; choose major by end of spring semester	Teach and monitor college skills, time management, organization; coach on how to find and interact with services on campus
	9	Increase self-awareness and knowledge of autism ***Complete Autism Project***	Complete final project, readings	Direct project and readings and monitor and refer as needed

Model One Components

Component	Description	Units
Intake Interview	One-on-one or small group Disability advocate and student/allies	1. Students who identify themselves to a disability advocate are asked if they wish to participate in a 2- to 3-hour orientation 2. If they say "yes," they will be given information, a date, and a time. If "no," nothing more is done. 3. If "yes," students are given one or more data-gathering tools during the interview. 4. The interview is completed, flyers are handed out, and reminder emails are set up.
Follow-Up Workshop	Group Students with autism and disability advocate	1. When I explain my autism and ask for support, I . . . 2. When I manage my time, I . . . 3. When I am in class, I . . . 4. When I study, I . . . 5. When I have sensory issues on campus, I . . . 6. When I socialize or talk to peers, I . . .

Model Two Components

Component	Description	Units
Orientation Week	Intensive 7- to 10-day orientation before the beginning of classes to establish college routine in academic context	Student Criteria for Success Disability Services Learning Styles Code of Conduct Getting Organized What Is Autism Anyway? Disability Disclosure Student–Instructor Advocacy Transportation Strategies How to Get Good Grades in College Student Activities Jeopardy Top Ten From My Point of View (Mind-Blindness) Zoom In; Zoom Out (Context Blindness)
One-on-Ones: Academic Coaching Sessions	Weekly sessions individualized for student success	Sessions are based on checklists and discussion and are individualized according to student need and insights as the semester(s) go forward
Plenary Group	Weekly group sessions to assist students in understanding what autism is and how it affects them as a college student and young adult	Three "moves" in the arch of the year Getting used to the demands of college (10 weeks): Advocacy, academics, friendship, and dating What's in your future? (5 weeks): Creating a realistic future plan; linking to adult services Finding your voice (5 weeks): Culminating biography project of successful adult with autism

Sample Orientation Week Schedule

	M 12th (1)	T 13th (2)	W 14th (3)	H 15th (4)	F 16th (5)	M 19th (6)	T 20th (7)
9:00	Intros & Photos CR	"Helping Students With Autism" (Brown)	The "How Will I Know?" (Wilson)	Circles Exercise (Wilson)	**IS** How to Get Good Grades	Social Skills Menu (Baker)	**TS** College Success Assessment
9:30	**IS** College Confidence Survey	**DA** Disability Services Overview	**IS** Getting Organized	**TS** Disability Disclosure		**AV** Advising	**IS & Profs.** "From My Point of View"
10:00	**IS** Student Criteria for Success	Former Student Q&A					
10:30		**IS** Code of Conduct 1					
11:00	**MW** Wright State Video		**IS** Code of Conduct 2 Quiz	**IS & TS** Scripts		**IS** Student Activities	**BM** National Science Foundation Grants
11:30			Lt. DB Public Safety	**IS** Transportation Issues	**IS** List of Questions		**IS** College Confidence Survey

12:00	Lunch	Lunch	Lunch	Lunch	Lunch	Lunch	Lunch
1:00	Personality Self-Score (Serebriakoff)	IS Learning styles	DF Working while a student	Campus Treasure Hunt	Library Tour Rm 302	Staff appts	Staff appts
1:30				Bookstore Pay Fees	1:1 with **IS** & **TS**	→	→
2:30	Walk thru classes, buildings, offices			Make ID		→	→
HW	Go over checklist for Orientation Week	Study for C of C quiz	Prioritize week 1–2	Skim booklets for "How to get good grades"	Go over Au 11 Checklist	Put appts on calendar	Complete checklists/calendar

AV: Academic Advisor

DA: Disability Services Advocate

IS: Intervention Specialist or College Disability Advocate

TS: Transition Specialist or College Admissions/First Year Advocate

Checklist for Starting a Student-Led Organization "of Interest in Autism"

❑ Find out the guidelines for student-led organizations at your college. Rules vary, but usually include requirements like obtaining a faculty sponsor and naming several officers. This information usually comes from a department with a name like "Student Support" or "Student Life." Frequently there is a dean's office associated with this part of a college.

❑ Create a strategic plan for your first three meetings prior to having your first meeting.

❑ Gather at least six to ten people who are interested. It is best if there are more students than faculty or staff, but at least one or two faculty or staff are usually required to "sponsor" an organization.

❑ Get each of them to invite one to three other people to the opening meeting.

❑ Make sure that at least one of the founding members really likes taking notes (or minutes) and ask that person to be the secretary, at least initially.

❑ Ask one person (can be faculty or student with experience) to lead the first meeting.

❑ Make the first meeting upbeat and open.

❑ If someone knows how to lead a brainstorming exercise or other creative idea-gathering activity, get them to do it. If not, try a website like http://thenextweb.com/lifehacks/2012/06/04/how-to-moderate-a-brainstorming-session/

❑ Keep an accurate list of the ideas, hopes, and concerns generated during this session.

❑ Before the first session ends, and while everyone is still there, schedule the next meeting.

❑ FOLLOW UP with each person face-to-face or by phone. Do not rely on email alone to help attendees remember what happened and what comes next.

❑ Get information out to the community as soon as possible on what this organization is, why they would want to join it, and when and how they can become involved.

FACULTY/STAFF RESOURCES

First Day Exercise

1. Introduce students to "cognitive maps" and ask them to each take a moment to draw a picture of the learning space. Don't be too specific about the directions. This will allow differences in perception, and the weight a person gives to certain features will to rise to the surface. For instance, someone may prominently include the class clock in their drawing, whereas others don't even notice the class has a clock. These are the kinds of features that lend themselves best to later discussion.

2. As an alternative, ask the students to finish this sentence: My favorite classroom space or learning environment... (This can be started orally, but in order to reach out to all students, not just the boldest or most verbal ones, provide a visual support for the discussion. This can be either up front on the board or a handout.) Allow students to draw features of a favorite classroom or learning environment as an alternative. Give plenty of time for each student to process and produce an answer.

3. Now ask students to carefully examine and describe the features of the learning space they are in right now. Again, provide visual support for their answers and enough time for each student to process and produce a description.

4. Compare their perceptions with the actual space, noting what features are in common to most as well as what features are unique to individuals. Connect this to perception.

5. Create a simple (five- or seven-point) Likert scale visually, orally, or physically (all stand in a line and move) that runs between "Hinders my learning process" to "Enhances my learning process." Then raise each described feature and ask students to rate it on the scale.

6. Invite students to "redesign" the space so it comes out better for everyone. Negotiate and honor differences (some may like the lighting whereas others hate it). Reality check their ideas, noting which may actually be implemented and which may not. (Speaking of lighting, for instance, it is possible to bring in other kinds of light to a classroom and shut off the overheads.)

7. End by using this as an illustration of how "invisible differences or preferences" affect adult learning and are as real and

important as differences based on race, gender, and other visible characteristics.

8. Invite anyone who has expressed an intellectual difference or sensory need, and those who might have one but have not publicly expressed it yet, to come to you or to put it on the paper they turn in. Promise to follow up. (Note: this is also a good time to do a plug for disability services and other supportive services on your campus.)

9. Follow up in private if possible, especially with those who spoke to you and with those who might have seemed a little more reluctant to "play." Sometimes, those are the students with autism.

Moving From Assumption to Acceptance— A Faculty/Staff Training

See This/Think That	Realize It's Autism (the Effects of the Autistic Condition)	Do This Instead
Poor eye contact/On drugs; did not do reading	Social challenges Sensory differences	Agree on an "I'm listening indicator"
Argumentativeness/ Rebellion; hormones	Special interests Literal/Concrete thinking Superior intellect	Use a parking lot
Rich vocabulary; poor use of language/Talking back	Literal/Concrete thinking Language construction	5-Minute meetings
Difficulty producing written work or notes/ Lazy; unmotivated	Sensory differences	Movement breaks Frontload the notes
Tendency to make irrelevant comments or interrupt/disrespectful	Social challenges Executive function deficits Special interests	30-Second think
Problems with personal space and social distance/ Rude, perverse	Social challenges	Model social space and how to ask for space (with autism students and neurotypicals)
You are encouraged to discuss and fill in these last two sections of the chart yourself: What might you do as an instructor to deal with a student who knows more than you do (as in the illustration about General Lee's horse)? As a student, what might you do to help someone be more successful with group work?		

Knows more than the instructor on their "special interests"/ Showing off, know-it-all	Superior intellect Special interests	
May have difficulty coping socially and emotionally in group projects/Antisocial	Executive function deficits Social challenges	

Column B and Column C are further explained as follows:

Moving From Assumption to Acceptance: Effects of the Autistic Condition (Column B)

- *Executive Function Deficits*—impulsivity, organization, time management
- *Literal/Concrete Thinking*—affects humor and general comprehension
- *Language Construction*—intonation, modulation, and syntax
- *Sensory Differences*—both hyper- and hyposensitivity
- *Social Challenges*—does not easily recognize another's point of view or the "hidden curriculum" in a social situation
- *Exemplary Intellect*—memory that is more accurate than peers or professor in a narrow area
- *Special Interests*—perceived as narrow and intense

Moving From Assumption to Acceptance: What Techniques May Be Helpful (Column C)

- *Agree on an "I'm Listening Indicator"*—This is a nonverbal way for the student and instructor to communicate that the student is paying attention. It can be the student's hand on a desktop or any other gesture that both agree on in lieu of eye contact or other neurotypical ways of showing interest.
- *Use a Parking Lot*—A "parking lot" is a section of the board where ideas or information brought up in class, but not immediately relevant to the lecture, may be written or "parked." This allows the instructor to complete the scope of his or her lecture and also validates the student's input or question. The class may return to the parking lot at the end of the lecture or on a later day.

- *5-Minute Meetings*—The student and instructor may agree to have regular 5-minute meetings before or after class or at alternative times in order to delve more deeply into a subject, clarify the notes, or otherwise review or reinterpret the information together.

- *Movement Breaks*—Many students, not just autistic ones, require physical releases or movement breaks from time to time. These can be as elaborate as leaving for a self-timed interval and returning or as simple and subtle as squeezing one's hands together under the desk—whatever works, as long as both the instructor and student agree it is not a distraction for the rest of the students.

- *Frontload the Notes*—Because many students are visual learners, it is helpful if they can receive notes ahead of the lecture time. It is important again that instructors approve of this. There are also regular accommodations that include volunteer note takers and the use of recording devices.

- *30-Second Think*—The 30-second think is a way of allowing all students to have adequate time to process a question. With this technique, the class is told that they are to each think of a response to a question that is coming up, and that they will all be given 30 seconds to do this. No one is to say anything before the time is called, then each student is encouraged to share their response. The use of a visual timer helps this work even better.

- *Model Social Space and How to Ask for Space (with autism students and neurotypicals)*—Many techniques exist on how to model social space for little ones; however, college-age people face new challenges regarding social space that they may have not had before. Ask both men and women to share what feels comfortable to them and what feels "sketchy" or even downright "creepy" when it comes to physical space. This will vary with the nature of the relationship between the people, but bringing it out into the open may help alleviate discomfort and social faux pas; it may even prevent issues pertaining to harassment. Note that at the minimum, students should be asked if they mind being touched by others. A light hand on the shoulder or arm may be OK for one but extremely threatening to another.

THREE SAMPLE LESSON PLANS FOR GROUP (PLENARY) MEETINGS

Lesson Plan 1. Check Your Scene: Formal and Informal Behavior in College

Outcome:	Student will be able to
	1. Identify what kind of setting(s) are found in college.
	2. Describe the difference between formal and informal behavior.
	3. Write a scenario from their own experience that demonstrates appropriate behavior (actions/language) within an identified setting.
Differentiation:	**Students' ability to use context to make meaning vary in this cohort. The lesson seeks to address this variance:**
	1. Students are matched with peers whose social skills competencies are more developed with those whose competencies are less developed. Competency is based on AVR ratings, Baker and Brown Assessment results given during Orientation Week, and observation.
	2. Visual support (use of handouts and projector) and sensory support (fidgets and movement) are incorporated into the lesson plan.
Procedure:	1. Students are reminded that appropriate behavior often comes from how a person reads the entire scene or setting, using an illustration from *Where's Waldo?*
	2. Each student comes forward and writes a different college setting on the board (total six).
	3. Students are introduced to the idea that there are two kinds of behavior—formal and informal—by looking at the adapted worksheet from the Baker text.
	4. Students break into pairs (one more socially competent, one still developing this competency) to discuss this difference.
	5. Pairs come forward and label the college settings on the board as either "formal" (bowtie) or "informal" (blue jeans) and report why they chose those labels.
	6. Class discusses the opinions and results together.
	7. Leader models a scenario that requires formal behavior and one that allows informal.
	8. Students write one scenario from their college experience so far that required formal behavior and one that allowed informal behavior and turn this writing in.

Assessment:	Completed visual aid; participation (one to three verbal comments per student); scenario write-ups
Materials:	"Formal Versus Informal Behavior" handout (adapted for college age); bowtie and blue jeans visual aids; whiteboard (or flip board); fidgets; timer

Sources: Baker, Jed. (2003). *Social Skills Training* (pp 142–143). Shawnee Mission, KS, AAPC; Vermeulen, Peter. (2012). *Autism as Context Blindness.* Shawnee Mission, KS: AAPC.

Check Your Scene Handout

	Formal	Informal
Definition	**Very Polite and Respectful**	**Casual and Relaxed**
People	Other adults you do not know well; authority figures like professors, group leaders, college staff, police, employers	Good friends and close family members
Greetings	"Hello, how are you?"	"What's up?" "How's it going?"
Speaking out	Signal you want to speak. When speaking, keep it brief and succinct. Notice how others are reacting to your words. Do not talk over others. Do not interrupt.	May interrupt sometimes. Ask, listen, respond with relevant follow-up questions. Seek to listen twice as much as you talk.
Listening position	Sit upright. Make eye contact. Quiet hands and feet (use hidden fidget if needed).	May sit in a more relaxed way. Pay attention to others' position and mirror it. Use eye contact when you can.
Deciding what to do	You can let the other person know what you would like, but the authority figure gets to decide.	Seek compromise so everyone can get some of what they want.
Jokes, bawdy behavior	No racial, sexual, or mean humor. Don't go there. Take the situation seriously. Tell clean jokes only if the authority figure does.	You can tell a joke if your friends want to hear it, but ask first. Stop immediately if your friends ask you to stop or if they look uncomfortable.

Practice

Write a scenario from your college experience so far that required *formal* behavior. Include the setting, the people involved, how you were expected to speak and listen, what happened, and how you think you did.

Write a scenario from your college experience so far that allowed you to have *informal* behavior. Include the setting, the people involved, how you were expected to speak and listen, what happened, and how you think you did.

Lesson Plan 2. What Joe College Knows

This exercise is designed for college students on the autism spectrum. It is an active lesson: they have to get up and interact. It touches on two major skills deficits that sometimes occur in people on the spectrum. The first is executive functioning—they need to locate, read, and work with their class syllabus and due dates. The second is social interaction—the students have to engage one another in conversation around these topics.

Directions: *Fill in the first column with each of your classes. Get out your syllabi and/or class schedule. Take this chart to someone else and go through each of the other columns telling them about that class. The other person takes notes and puts their initials in the box. Then reverse roles. They tell you about their classes and you take notes and initial.*

Class	What Topics Will Be Covered	How Graded (Tests, Labs, Papers)	One Thing I'm Looking Forward to Is:	The Next Assignment Is:

Class	What Topics Will Be Covered	How Graded (Tests, Labs, Papers)	One Thing I'm Looking Forward to Is:	The Next Assignment Is:

A simple checklist like the one below can be used by the teacher or coach to note how the student is doing on the two skills. This exercise can be done twice with different topics or once each semester and the results compared to see if they improve the second time around.

Date of Exercise: _____

Student	Executive Function Skill	✔	Social Interaction Skill	✔	Notes
Student One	Found syllabus		Started conversation		
	Topics correctly enunciated		Took turns		
	Understand and can explain grades		Checked that other understood		
	Etc.		Etc.		
Student Two	Found syllabus		Started conversation		
	Topics correctly enunciated		Took turns		
	Understand and can explain grades		Checked that other understood		
	Etc.		Etc.		

Lesson Plan 3. Photo Phone Scavenger Hunt: A Great Way to Get to Know the Campus Environment

After a campus (or building) tour, engage students on the spectrum in the process of getting to know their new environment. Divide into pairs or groups and have them do a photo phone scavenger hunt. You can record the results by making a chart or by putting together a quick slide show or PowerPoint of their images.

Students on the autism spectrum sometimes have difficulty navigating a new space at first—so pair them up carefully, maybe with a neurotypical student. Also, have each pair set a timer on their phone to keep them from drifting too long. Call them to bring them back in. Finally, this lesson can be tweaked to teach how to work in a group.

Scavenger Hunt Example

- ❏ Take a photo on your phone of each of the following. Be the first back to the room for a prize.
- ❏ The silent floor of the Library
- ❏ The Writing Center in the Library
- ❏ The *Star Trek* lounge on the second floor of the Humanities Building
- ❏ The computer lab
- ❏ The hallway-size aquarium on the top floor of the Science Building
- ❏ Student Union "loud lounge"
- ❏ Student Union "quiet lounge"
- ❏ Administrative Hall Counseling Center (basement)
- ❏ The roof courtyard on the top floor of the cafeteria
- ❏ The workout room in the Physical Education Hall
- ❏ The campus restaurant behind the cafeteria
- ❏ The founder's statue
- ❏ The sculptures on the Mall
- ❏ The weird bridge from north campus to the parking garage
- ❏ The solar panels from the base of the Administrative Hall

CPSIA information can be obtained
at www.ICGtesting.com
Printed in the USA
FFHW021413080619
52877567-58457FF